Sto

ROARING
F A I T H

Compiled and Edited By
Donna Skell
Belinda McBride ◆ Frank Ball ◆ Sherry Ryan

Roaring Lambs Publishing
17110 Dallas Pkwy Ste 260
Dallas, TX 75248

Phone: 972.380.0123
Email: info@RoaringLambs.org

RoaringLambs.org

Dedication

To God,
Thank You for the difference
You make in our lives.

To Garry Kinder,
Founder of Roaring Lambs Ministries,
Because of you, this book is possible.

To all the contributors of this book,
Thank you for sharing your personal testimonies
With the world.

To all the readers,
May your relationship
With our Lord Jesus Christ grow.

Table of Contents

Introduction _____ 1

Foreword: The Power of Story _____ 3

From Abused to Anointed by Stephanie Jane Martino _____ 5

Each Day Is a Gift by Mark Cragle _____ 12

Suffering to Restoration by Elizabeth Dyer Covard _____ 21

Wins, Losses, and Firsts by Joyce Brown _____ 29

Searching for Home by Vivien Chambers _____ 37

Twenty-Seven Hours of Agony by Melinda Propes_____ 45

I Am the Woman at the Well by Mayada Naami _____ 53

Falling Off the Radar by Jenni Eastin _____ 59

A Recycled Life by Dee Gibbs _____ 64

My True Name by Sarah Pittmann _____ 72

The Hole in My Heart by Heather Dennis _____ 80

Buffering by Cheri McKean _____ 88

Mental Illness and a Near-Miss Bullet by Debra Moore _____ 95

Standing before the Mirror by Majeedah Murad _____ 106

Beautifully Molded by Starlet Bell _____ 115

Hewn from an Ozark Rock by Mark Tohlen_____ 122

The Ticking Alarm Clock by Michele Stevens _____ 130

Seeds of Faith by Mark Dann _____ 136

No One Believed Me by Kim Lakin Creger _____ 141

My Thorn in the Flesh by William Comer_____ 148

The Lake and the Holy Spirit by Sue Z. McGray _____153

Never Give Up by Cathy Kilpatrick_____160

In the Making by Tobi Adeyemi _____165

Finding Peace in War by Lara Lorena Cardoso Zwahlen ___174

Sink or Swim by Diane Claire _____183

Seasons of Change by Cherie Nichols _____191

Breaking the Rules by Connie Steindorf _____198

Overcoming the Power of the Evil One by Cathy Birungi __204

Learning to Trust God by Betty Willis_____211

Anti-Virus Protection by Juanita Williams _____221

Beliefs from God's Word _____228

God's Good News for You_____229

Share with Us _____230

Support Us _____231

Acknowledgments_____232

About the Editors _____233

Introduction

About thirty-five years ago, I had the opportunity to attend a small class that taught me how to confidently and effectively share the gospel against the backdrop of my life experiences. **It changed my life.** I learned the importance of sharing how God had proved Himself real to me.

Come and hear, all you who fear God; let me tell you what he has done for me. — Psalm 66:16

For the last several years, Roaring Lambs has been encouraging and equipping believers to effectively compose their testimony. Whether sharing one-on-one, speaking to a group, or just putting it in writing as a legacy for future generations, it is beneficial.

We will tell the next generation the praiseworthy deeds of the Lord, his power, and the wonders he has done, so the next generation would know them, even the children yet to be born, and they in turn would tell their children. — Psalm 78:4, 6

Our testimony is our opportunity to let God use the circumstances He has allowed in our life for His glory. When you can take a difficult time, show how God used it for His good and yours, then you can give Him glory for that very hardship.

When he heard this, Jesus said, "This sickness will not end in death. No, it is for God's glory so that God's Son may be glorified through it." — John 11:4

Putting your faith story together will prepare you for many opportunities to share your faith. Each day, you are more likely to realize just how many there are.

But in your hearts revere Christ as Lord. Always be prepared to give an answer to everyone who asks you to give the reason for the hope that you have. But do this with gentleness and respect. — 1 Peter 3:15

The world needs to see how real Jesus is. Times are short. Your story matters. It is the living water that others need.

Then he said to his disciples, "The harvest is plentiful but the workers are few." — Matthew 9:37

Are you ready to be used by God and be richly blessed? Tell your story of what He has done for you.

Then I heard the voice of the Lord saying, "Whom shall I send and who will go for us?" And I said, "Here am I. Send me." — Isaiah 6:8

Donna Skell, Executive Director
Roaring Lambs

Foreword: The Power of Story

Everywhere I go, I have to tell my story.

As a devout Jew, I was working so hard to make everything right, when actually I was only doing what was right in my own eyes. There is a way that seems right to men, but it leads to death instead of life. I was walking such a path, seeking to destroy the very thing that was my source of life.

With arrest warrants in my hand, I was on a mission to arrest anyone of the heretical sect who followed this Jesus, who was dead. Crucified. End of story. At least that's what should have been true. It would have been if those deceived people would accept the truth. Instead, they believed Jesus was alive, raised from the dead. Jewish leaders had plenty of evidence to convince them otherwise, but they weren't listening.

I was just outside the city, leading six men who would infiltrate the communities, find their leaders, and arrest them. Suddenly I was surrounded by blinding light like I was staring directly into the sun. I fell to my knees and bowed to the ground, trying to shield myself, yet the brilliance remained, even with my eyes closed.

A voice like thunder shook the ground. "Why are you persecuting me?"

"Sir, who are you?" I opened my eyes, but saw nothing but the light.

"I am Jesus," the voice said. "How hard it is for you to resist my prodding."

I was trembling, feeling too weak to stand. "What do you want me to do?"

"Get up," Jesus said. "Go into the city, and you'll be told what to do."

One of my men took my hand, asking if I was all right. His words sounded like whispers compared to the thunderous voice still ringing in my ears.

"Did you see that? Did you hear what he said?"

They had seen only a flash of lighting. They heard thunder.

That was all, which made no sense. On the way, I had seen no clouds, not even in the distance.

They led me by the hand to a room on Straight Street. I couldn't see the path in front of me. I couldn't see the city walls, the sky, not anything. All I could see was the light.

For three days, I prayed. I ate no food. I drank no water. I had only those words playing like trumpets in my ears. "I am Jesus. Why are you persecuting me?" There was no denying the truth. Jesus was alive. How could I have been so wrong? If Jesus was alive, then he did rise from the dead. And the Jews' story about his body being stolen had to be a lie.

I was visualizing the rest of my life as a blind man when a vision came through the light. A man named Ananias appeared in the vision, laid his hands upon me, and my sight was restored. Later, when a stranger walked in and introduced himself as the one I had seen in the vision, I felt cold chills that warmed my heart. Tears came to my eyes as he explained his reluctance to come, but Jesus had told him exactly where to find me and what to say.

"Brother Saul," he said, "The Lord Jesus, who appeared to you on the way here, has sent me that you might be filled with the Holy Spirit and receive your sight."

If I had more time, I could give you more details. If you are a Jew, I can give you word after word from the Law and the Prophets that prove the truth. Jesus is the sought-after Messiah who came, not to establish an earthly kingdom but to give us his Spirit, change our hearts, and make us part of his family.

Everywhere I go, I tell this story so others can meet Jesus as I did. They get to see the light as I did, hear Jesus' voice, and know he is real.

I don't know what your story is, but if you met Jesus and your life was changed, you have a story that also needs to be told. People will get to see the light as you did, hear Jesus' voice, and know he is real.

That's the power of story.

By Saul of Tarsus, also known as Paul, called to be an apostle

From Abused to Anointed
by Stephanie Jane Martino

"Jesus loves the little children, all the children of the world."

Really? All the children in the world? Hmm. As a child, I didn't feel loved by God. *Maybe God loves me like the love demonstrated around me. Maybe God disciplines me like my father, who physically abuses me in the name of discipline. Or maybe God loves me like my stepfather, who regularly sexually and physically abuses me. Or maybe, just maybe, God's forgiveness is as fake as the prayers for forgiveness I am forced to pray after my stepfather finishes sexually abusing me.*

Because of the horrific abuse I endured as a child, I had a distorted view of God. I always said, "If anything bad can happen to me, it will happen." I hated being a child. I certainly didn't like the idea of being a child of God. I desperately wanted to grow up, get out of my parents' homes, and be responsible for myself. My family taught me what not to be. My family hurt the people they loved by demonstrating rage and anger. I had to be careful not to upset others, because their punishment, also known as discipline, was extreme.

I didn't often play with dolls, because I didn't know what nurturing family relationships looked like. I was a tomboy, busy climbing trees, running around, or reading books. I despised being a pretty little girl so much that I butchered my long blond hair twice.

My family took me to church, but I didn't trust God. I didn't think He saw me or listened to my prayers. I thought I was a dirty little girl, because I aroused my stepfather's anger. His beatings, even at three years old, caused me intense pain. My stepfather claimed he would kill me if I let anyone know. I hated him.

By the grace of God, when I was nine years old, my sister and I told our father's girlfriend about the abuse. As a result, my stepfather left our lives for good. Unfortunately, my abuse continued through different people and in different places. I couldn't find anywhere safe.

Somehow, this abused little girl who was raised in the church read the Bible from Genesis to Revelation. When I was finished,

I asked Jesus into my life on October 21, 1990, and was baptized on January 13, 1991. I loved reading my Bible.

In this world, we have trials and troubles. A few months after I asked Jesus to be my Savior, I was raped. Then I was jumped. This later beating was different because the perpetrator broke my front tooth. At fourteen, one of the only things I liked when I looked in the mirror was my smile. My top teeth were naturally perfect. My tooth was the last part of me to be marred. I felt shattered.

Satan is more evil than anything I can comprehend. He worked hard at keeping my mind clouded from the truth. I questioned God. I asked Him things like, *How could You let this happen? I was being faithful to You. I love You, God, but why don't You love me?* I became angry with God and stopped reading my Bible. I started doing things that angered Him.

I delved into astrology, white magic, tarot cards, and different types of new-age spirituality. I knew God was sovereign, but I no longer believed He was good. I blamed Him for evil. I didn't want to pray anymore. Somehow surrendering to evil felt good, but my emotions were a mess and my depression got worse. None of the drugs I got my hands on masked my pain.

By the age of sixteen, I had moved fifteen times. Child Protective Services required two of those moves. I decided I was done bouncing around from Mom's house to Dad's to Grandma's, then back to Mom's or Dad's.

When I was finally old enough to drop out of school and live on my own, I thought I could keep myself safe, but I couldn't keep safe from myself. The first couple of years didn't go well. I was angry, bitter, felt lost, and took drugs. I didn't care.

I was flooded with emotions and often expressed them by writing. I was talented at making my pain sound rhythmic. It came to life when I shared my writings at poetry readings. I grasped the dark side of myself, yet had no idea how I was going to survive another day.

At seventeen, I lost all hope. I had reached the end. I was done. I was broken and didn't think I could be fixed. Brokenness was all I knew. I was afraid of everything. I hated myself. I didn't want to live anymore. I gave up.

That's when God stepped in. He wrapped His perfect, pure,

and holy love around me like a blanket. All my fear was gone. Everything was perfect at that moment. His glory surrounded me. He told me He had plans to prosper me and not to harm me, plans for a hope and a future.

With God's love and glory wrapped around me, I knew in an instant that I had the wrong idea about God. He showed me His love when I needed it most. I had lived in shame and thought I was too dirty, but God met me in my darkest hour. At last, I truly accepted being a child of God.

With this change, I started reading my Bible again. I understood that Satan kills, steals, and destroys. God doesn't. So I stopped blaming Him. I didn't know how He was going to make my life prosper, but I wanted the Bible to be my standard for living. I didn't know when God was going to heal my wounds, but I had faith that He would. Little by little, He changed my heart, my thoughts, and my will. I wondered if the sadness would ever disappear. Today I rejoice.

My purest heart cry was to be healthy and whole. I prayed that one day God would allow me to have a healthy family, one without abuse and one where my children were loved unconditionally.

He blessed me with a husband and two wonderful children. My husband is loyal to our family and is my safe place. His humor is a blessing, because laughter is important for healing deep, messy wounds. Healing is hard on the survivor, but it's also hard on the spouse. It's not easy to walk alongside someone while they heal, but the bond that is built through the power of Jesus is precious.

Once I learned to submit to God's way for marriage, true intimacy was possible. Unsure of how to balance my emotions, flashbacks, and being a wife, I sometimes tried to sabotage my marriage. Some memories caused me to be disgusted with myself, and I didn't want to be touched or intimate with my husband. Although incorrect, I knew my feelings were valid. I felt that I should want to hold my husband and be intimate with him. But I didn't know how.

God gave me eyes to see that my way wasn't always right. When I was a child, He also gave me eyes to see that my environment wasn't healthy. Now, I realized I was not in a healthy environment because of me.

I needed to heal on a deep level and forgive those who had wounded me. I needed to let go of the anger I was carrying. I had to stop telling myself I was all right and be honest with God about the emotions I was running from. I needed to fall in love with being a child of God. I had to surrender my marriage to God and do what He told me.

When I did this, my harshness disappeared. My bitter resentment, which was a heavy stone on my shoulders, slowly became a pebble that rolled off. Today, I have complete freedom that can only be found in Christ.

What are your top fears? Cancer? Not being able to pay your bills? Are you afraid of love, commitment, or being alone? Some people have a fear of clowns. Others are terrified of spiders. Most people have unspoken fears, the kind that Satan doesn't want you to expose. With the fear of saying the wrong thing, you don't say anything at all.

Self-awareness can cripple us if we don't take our fears to the Lord. We must know who God says we are so we can become the courageous child of God Who resides inside of us.

Because of my deep-seated fears, I questioned everything, even good decisions. Has fear ever stopped you from doing something that would be considered healthy? Because I feared the unknown early in my marriage, I didn't want to be intimate with my husband. My heart was calloused, and it took time for it to become tender. The more I trusted God's hand on my life, the easier it became to let my heart be open and vulnerable. Eventually, I was able to give my heart freely to my husband. God's perfect love drives out all fears.

Jesus put great importance on children. Matthew 18:3 says, "Unless you change and become like little children, you will never enter the Kingdom of Heaven."

Satan tries to deceive and take away God's glory, but as an abused child of God, I have found great comfort in the next verses. Matthew 18:6–7 says, "If anyone causes one of these little ones—those who believe in me—to stumble, it would be better for them to have a large millstone hung around their neck and to be drowned in the depths of the sea. Woe to the world because of the things that cause people to stumble! Such things must come, but woe to the person through whom they come!"

Jesus will judge the people who wounded me. God didn't call me to bitterness. He called me to forgiveness. I released the grip my abusers' sin had on me. Jesus died on a cross for all the sins of the world. Mark 11:25 says, "And when you stand praying, if you hold anything against anyone, forgive them, so that your Father in Heaven may forgive you your sins." I don't want anything to hinder my relationship with God.

Psalm 51:10 was my daily prayer one year. "Create in me a pure heart, O God, and renew a steadfast spirit within me."

Daily, God brought things to my mind, including incorrect thought patterns, attitudes, and actions that didn't align with God's Word. I learned to stop when I had a negative thought and seek His direction.

One day, God showed me that I didn't fully trust His protection. The next morning Psalm 124:2–3, 8 came to life. "If the Lord had not been on our side when people attacked us, they would have swallowed us alive when their anger flared against us. Our help is in the name of the Lord, the Maker of Heaven and Earth."

At that moment, I had clarity that my situations could have destroyed me, but Jesus had a path to freedom. He had a plan for my life that wouldn't harm me if only I chose to be faithful in believing He could work a miracle in me. I had to obey His leading and trust Him with everything.

I learned that Jesus saves the children of God, not only from eternal separation from Him, but He gives daily salvation from the evil one. James: 4:7–8 says, "Submit yourselves, then, to God. Resist the devil and he will flee from you. Come near to God and He will come near to you. Wash your hands, you sinners, and purify your hearts, you double-minded."

Healing with Jesus normally doesn't happen overnight. It's a moment-by-moment walk with Jesus. You must listen to the perfect questions He speaks to your heart. Answer them honestly, even when the answer hurts.

I was wounded deeply when He allowed me to see how the abuse caused me to sin. I wasn't the mother or wife God called me to be, because I walled off so many areas of my heart. I had to learn to be tender, patient, and loving in the way Jesus wanted.

Today I stand proud that I am a child of God, because the power of the cross heals. Jesus anointed me with His supernatural grace to forgive every person who wounded me. He came to Earth to save the lost. I was incredibly lost. He became human so He could understand our pain and suffering.

I didn't trust anyone with my wounded heart. However, Jesus is a life-giving source, and His mercy is new every morning. God has given His children the keys to Heaven to be with Him eternally, but we must accept Him as Savior and Lord. I was abused. Now I am an anointed child of God. You can be too.

Stefanie Jane Martino is a singer, speaker, and storyteller who speaks truthfully from the heart. She is a trained advocate for sexual abuse survivors. In 2009, Stefanie Jane released her album, See Me Change?, *which walks listeners through her path of healing. She uses her talents to shine God's light on this dark subject. In all the positions God places her in, Stefanie loves to share her hope in healing through Jesus Christ. Stefanie is a good communicator and leads Bible studies for survivors in the Dallas area, where she resides with her husband, Brian. Contact her at* **StefanieJane.com** *or* **Stefanie@StefanieJane.com.**

Thoughts to Ponder
from From Abused to Anointed

1. Jesus wants to meet you at your place of need.

2. Courage comes from knowing who God says you can be.

3. Your heavenly Father loves you like a warm blanket.

What truths do you believe about yourself?

Yet to all who did receive Him, to those who believed in His name, He gave the right to become children of God. — John 1:12

Each Day Is a Gift
by Mark Cragle

You never know what each day will bring.

A police car suddenly turned in front of me on the highway, and I had no time to hit the brakes. *Bam!* I smashed into the car going fifty miles an hour. My head hit the windshield. The shattered glass hurled sharp projectiles into my lips and pushed my teeth back. The battery exploded, spewing acid across my back.

I was driving home from a college night class. Because my car would not start that day, my parents loaned me their sturdy pickup truck. The fact that I was driving a big vehicle may have saved my life.

Two men stopped and pried the door open to get me out. I wandered around aimlessly, drifting in and out of shock. When I regained some cognition, I tried in vain to open the policeman's door, because no one had helped him out yet.

The ambulances took both of us to a small hospital. On the way there, I asked how the other driver was. To comfort me, they told me he was going to be okay. I had never been in an ambulance before, and the pain felt like a bucking bronco was kicking me. My head and body smashed into the dashboard, and my ribs wrapped around the steering wheel.

When I was in the examination room for a CAT scan, my brother told me the other driver had died at the scene, and they would be testing me for alcohol. That was not an issue, because I had not been drinking. Later I learned that I had suffered a concussion. In the small emergency waiting room, only my family and police officer Malcom Strong's family were in the room. Less than an hour earlier, any betting person would have said it was the twenty-one-year-old kid's fault, not the respected police officer's.

What happened next was a milestone. My mother talked to Mrs. Strong, who just found out that her husband of fifty years had died. She told Mrs. Strong how sorry she was for her loss. Mrs. Strong lived up to her last name and said, "If someone had to die, I am glad it was not your son. Malcom lived a great life, and he is in Heaven now."

Who responds that way when they just suffered a major loss? Very few.

Mrs. Strong's grace and faith changed my search for God from wanting to find Him to realizing how much I needed Him. Previously, I thought I could get to God on intellect alone or at least by being a good person.

I grew up in a home where we went to church occasionally. I knew there was a God but did not have a relationship with Him. My father was a mean-spirited man and cheated on my mother when my brother and I were infants. I grew up wanting to be nothing like my father. My parents were always at each other's throats. My mother did the best she could to raise her three sons. Growing up, I was a decent kid and did not get into much trouble. However, my home life was like being in a log-rolling contest where I struggled to stay on the log.

As a teenager, I went to a few church services and started listening to Christian music. The seeds were planted in my heart to recognize my need for God. There is a song called, *I'm Not Lucky, I'm Loved*. The words rang true for me, *I have had more sunshine than rain*. The sunshine is the easy part of one's life. The rain can make you stronger and bring you closer to Jesus. That is exactly what the car accident and Mrs. Strong's strength did for me. It brought me to Jesus. Mrs. Strong allowed God to use the tragedy of her husband's death for His triumph and glory. I wanted what Mrs. Strong possessed. Shortly thereafter, I prayed, confessed my sins, and acknowledged Jesus as Lord and Savior.

Later, I got married. At the age of 28, my wife and I lost our stillborn baby girl at nine months of pregnancy. In Scripture, Jesus says He will be with us until the end of the age. He kept His promise.

Because of a job opportunity, my wife, two wonderful sons, and I moved from Rochester, New York, to Dallas, Texas. When I grew up, I was a Dallas Cowboys fan, so I was excited about moving to Texas, and I was glad to move away from the Snow Belt. The first year was great until I became materialistic. Marital problems and divorce followed. I felt like I let God and my sons down. Eventually, I remarried a wonderful woman named Teri and finally figured out what true love is. She became a grounding force for me.

Another milestone occurred in the summer of 2010. As I was waiting at the lake to test drive a jet ski, I noticed a woman flailing in the water. I thought she might be drowning. So I ran down the boat ramp. When I hit the edge of the water, it was slippery with wet moss, and my feet slid from underneath me. *Boom!* I fell backward and the back of my head smashed violently into the cement, whiplashing and cracking bones in my neck. In that instant, my life severely changed.

My brain sheared from inside my skull in three places. The neurologist told me I had a 50 percent chance of survival, and if there were four shears that were detached from my brain, I would die. However, once again God was with me, and I lived. For years, I suffered memory loss, dizziness, slurring of words, eye focus issues, and extreme pain. Socializing became tough, and brain overload sometimes led to my shutting down.

Previously, I had been an outgoing, smiling person. Now, concentration was an issue. People seemed to avoid me, probably because I looked mad, which was seldom the case. Instead, my demeanor was due to chronic head pain, orders of magnitude greater than a severe headache. One of the side-effects of pain medicine was suicidal ideation. I didn't want to die, but the medicine was telling me to get a gun and blow my brains out. God was with me then as well, because He showed me that I had worth. He revealed that it was the medicine or evil telling me otherwise. Trials are part of our lives. We weaken our spirit when we fear and lose our hope. However, we are strengthened in spirit, faith, and hope when we call on God to help us face our trials and overcome them.

I started meeting with a Stephens minister, Sabir, who was a layperson trained to help people in crisis. He met with me one-on-one and offered encouragement and support. Sabir asked, "Are you angry with God?"

I was not, but I did wonder, *Why did I fall and have a brain injury, Lord, when I was trying to help that woman struggling in the water?* However, according to Isaiah 55:8, "For My thoughts are not Your thoughts, neither are Your ways My ways, declares the Lord." While I don't understand, I also know He has blessed me in many ways.

14

One of those blessings was when Teri and I volunteered with our church's special needs program. That put many things in perspective. Money and material objects became less important. Those kids, primarily with Down syndrome and autism, were happy and kind most of the time, despite having a disease all of their lives. I learned a lot from these kids. God, family, friends, the special needs ministry, and my Stephens minister, Sabir, gave me grounding, joy, faith, and boldness.

June 1, 2018, was another day that rocked my world. I went to my neurologist to get what I thought was a routine visit on the status of my annual MRI that monitored my traumatic brain injury. They told me I have a rare brain disease called Cerebral Amyloid Angiopathy (CAA), which is a protein that builds up in the blood vessels and tears through the vessels causing blood, protein, and iron to be deposited on my brain.

A deadly bleeding stroke was my immediate risk, with a 13 percent survival rate, and if I survived, severe brain damage including blindness, paralysis, seizures, and eventually, vascular dementia. The doctor said, "Other than controlling your blood pressure, there is no treatment or cure. Go and try to live your life." How does someone deal with bad news sprung on you like that? It was like the weight of the world was instantly put on me. I was numb and spent the next few months trying to convince people that there was no cure, because their initial response was, "Surely something can be done." One day you are *status quo* and the next you are told you have an incurable brain disease. We don't put our trust in mankind, only the Creator of mankind.

I spent many hours researching, trying to find doctors who treated CAA and arranging appointments. I went to the best clinics in the country, including the Mayo Clinic and UT Southwestern. They told me, "Nothing can be done. You're in God's hands now." I was blessed to find the best doctor in the world on this disease at Mass General Hospital (MGH) in Boston: Dr. Greenberg.

He went through all nine of my MRI's that showed the progressions from three bleeds on the first MRI from the lakeside injury to the fifty I have currently. Three bleeds are life-threatening, and Dr. Greenberg told me the average is twelve. I asked him, "Why am I still alive?" I did not receive an answer.

He also said I have a second incurable brain disease called Cortical Superficial Siderosis which is a pooling of the blood. Another doctor called me a ticking time bomb.

The next four months after diagnosis were terrible—with stroke-like symptoms, limb jerking, swallowing issues, facial numbness, stumbling, gait issues, anxiety, chronic pain, brain fog, cognitive issues, and three trips to the emergency room. I am thankful to God that I did not have a stroke. I realized that every day could be my last.

A pivotal day in my journey with the Lord was around July 4, a month after diagnosis. I prayed, "Lord, I am broken. I don't know if I will live another day. You probably can't use me, but if You can, please do."

Before my diagnosis, Teri and I made plans to go on a church trip to follow the footsteps of the apostle Paul in Greece. Two days before we were supposed to leave, I had an episode while eating lunch at Jason's Deli. I thought I was having another bleed or a massive stroke and was going to die, right there on the floor in front of my wife in a crowded restaurant. We almost canceled our trip to Greece but decided to go anyway.

We did not know forty-five of the fifty people on the trip. The first three days were bad. On day four, God showed His mercy. Teri and I were re-baptized where the apostle Paul baptized many people 2,000 years ago. After that, a woman who knew about my sickness came forward and the group prayed for me.

One hour later, a picture of Teri and me was taken in front of the ancient Philippi city ruins. The picture showed a ray of light coming down from the clouds and landing directly on my head. The next ten days or so, I became stronger. Prayer works. I believe God showed me favor. It was no coincidence that our itinerary followed the apostle Paul's journey as he boldly proclaimed his faith despite suffering and trials. This trip, and my suffering, brought me closer to God. The Bible tells me the suffering we have in this world isn't worthy to be compared to the glory yet to come. He promises us blessings in the middle of pain.

We returned to Dallas after the trip, and I had another MRI. It was the first one in nearly ten years, with no new bleeds. It made me realize that each day is a gift. We are not promised tomorrow.

The Lord has blessed me with two terrific sons, their wives, and two grandsons. My youngest grandson is Max, whom I thought I would never meet. The purpose of this life is simple. Learn to walk with Jesus on Earth and be with Him in Heaven when this life is over. I also realize you can't take material things with you when you die. However, you can take others.

Without God and support from others, I could not have come this far. He gives me peace that passes all understanding. I still have the bleeds, but since that prayer in Greece, my symptoms and progression have reduced. My question on the meaning of life has been answered. We are only here for a season, and eternity is forever. The Bible says in 2 Corinthians 4:18, "So we fix our eyes not on what is seen, but on what is unseen, since what is seen is temporary, but what is unseen is eternal." This world and my body are temporal, but my spirit is eternal. The real question is where do you want to spend eternity?

God spurred me on to fight this disease with everything I can and to be used by Him. I pray He lets me stay a little longer to positively influence my two grandsons, Zander and Max. I want the youngest, Max, to remember me.

I was told if your story does not reveal the depth of your pain, the message is shallow. Upon diagnosis, I decided to be transparent and share my story with others. I was a software salesperson, and I am not a counselor, medically trained, or an expert on Scripture. I invested hundreds of hours learning about CAA and have gained extensive knowledge about this disease, as well as dementia, stroke, diet, and more.

I have spoken with, emailed, and messaged caregivers and patients from all over the USA, England, Ireland, Australia, and recently Zimbabwe. Most of these people say they have no hope and do not have adequate medical care simply because of income, where they live, or the scarcity of knowledgeable doctors. Some say, "If I have no hope, I just want to die."

I created a packet of information to send people with chronic illnesses, on things they can do to help with their condition and to find joy every day. I feel humbled and blessed that God uses me to help others. It is not through my power or intelligence but only through God's power and grace. In the past eighteen months, my prayer for God to use me has been answered beyond my wildest expectations. For example:

- A seventy-one-year-old man told me that his wife struggled with three to four seizures per week. After I shared information with him, he called back the next day and thanked me because his wife slept better than she had in three years. Recently he called and told me that in the last six months she has not had a seizure.

- A sixty-two-year-old woman in Australia recently diagnosed with CAA, who is also the caregiver for her husband with Alzheimer's, told me she learned more from me in two days than from her doctors in five months. I shared God and prayed with her.

- A man from Boston called me, because on various forums he felt that I was one of the few who try to encourage and not just say, "Why bother? I will be dead soon." At the end of the conversation, he said, "I have not prayed in fifteen years, but it's time to start."

- I've worked with Dr. Greenberg at MGH and have created two fundraisers for research. I was humbled and honored to be spotlighted in his newsletter, chosen from 1,000 patients. He knows I take what I learn from him and share it with the less fortunate. I have his cell number, and he has thanked me for all I do. He knows it's God working through me. I am presently working as an advocate, including preparing a letter to send to U.S. Senators for awareness and funding for this disease. It's paying it forward. In Matthew 25:40, God says, "Whatever you did for one of the least of these brothers and sisters of Mine, you did for Me."

- Exercise is very important for me, and I wear Christian-related hats and shirts. I wear a medical bracelet that people ask me about. One shirt simply says, "Drops in the Ocean." When that stirs a conversation, I say, "God loves you more than the drops in the ocean."

- I often feel led to share Jesus with others and pray for sick people.

God answers prayers. It is humbling to let other people see our weaknesses, share our suffering, and bear others' burdens. It is an act of love and grace. God can use us even when we think He can't.

Like me, He can use you in a broken state and give you a sense of purpose and peace. Psalm 139 says all the days that were ordained for me were written in His book before one of them ever happened. He brings me opportunities to serve Him. I never know what each day will bring, but I consider each day a gift.

Mark Cragle is a blogger and retired Field Sales Engineer. He earned his mechanical engineering degree at Rochester Institute of Technology and worked in that field for many years while living in upstate New York. Mark is married to Teri, and they have two married sons and two adorable grandsons. He likes to volunteer by working with special needs children at his church and being an advocate for people who suffer from brain diseases and injuries.

Thoughts to Ponder
from Each Day Is a Gift

1. Difficult circumstances can bring you closer to Jesus.

2. This world and your body are temporal but your spirit is eternal.

3. God can use your tragedy for His triumph.

> ## What events have altered the course of your life?

The Lord has done it this very day;
let us rejoice today and be glad. — Psalm 118:24

Suffering to Restoration
by Elizabeth Dyer Covard

"Mr. Gorbachev, tear down this wall."

Those words were spoken by President Reagan in 1987. He was speaking to the leader of the Communist Party of the Soviet Union. The wall had separated East and West Berlin since 1961, and he felt it was time to restore the city to unity. Just a few years after that speech, I visited Berlin to see the restoration for myself. It was very slow progress. When the wall fell, East Berlin was a stark contrast to its counterpart, West Berlin. The progress was slow, but the restoration moved steadily eastward.

Do you like watching home-remodel shows? Restoration and risks are often found in these TV shows. Walls are torn down and built back up. Either entire plumbing systems are replaced, or the electrical lines are ripped out. These restoration projects seem impossible to complete, but in just forty-eight minutes, the home is magnificent.

I love the restoration stories in the Bible too. In the books of Ruth and Job, or in the life of the apostle Paul, lives are transformed.

Ruth and Naomi found restoration in two different ways. One became an ancestor of Christ the Messiah, and the other tore down the walls of bitterness to see God's hand of grace and mercy.

Job seemed to have everything until tragedy took his children, his home, and his livestock. God replaced Job's losses with double what was lost. Job trusted God even when his wife said he should curse God and die.

The apostle Paul persecuted believers, but through a blinding experience with God, he became a believer. Even though he was a believer, Paul's new life included beatings, jail time, shipwrecks, and strained relationships.

Through these examples, we learn that God works in ways we never expect.

In my life, restoration began in 2013. During the months following the loss of my husband, friends encouraged me to start a blog. As I searched for creative names for the blog, I found a name I loved. The problem was, it was already taken. I investigated the ministry site and found it to be amazing— exactly the type of ministry and site for widows that I wanted to create. They were receiving submissions for guest posts. With all its flaws and rabbit trails, I submitted my story for consideration. Not only was it accepted for publication, but later I was asked to join the ministry team. God has since provided many opportunities to tell my story of loss and restoration.

Through the use of social media, conferences, and retreats, God has given me opportunities I never dreamed of. Never before had I written, and the only public speaking I had done was teaching in a classroom. Now, these pieces came together to point to God's power in me. I took a risk to share my story, and God brought me restoration by allowing my voice to help others who were going through similar journeys.

One day my phone buzzed. A widow-sister I had known for many years had lost her husband to cancer, leaving her with a preschooler and a baby. She became part of our prayer group.

For many years, she prayed for another group member whose wife was ill. Even though they didn't know each other, she mentioned at the prayer fellowships that she was praying for them. When his wife succumbed to her illness, my friend went to the funeral. She took a risk, showing up at a funeral of someone she hadn't even met. That's how caring she was.

Since the funeral attendees packed the church, this husband was unable to thank everyone for coming. He decided to make a spreadsheet of everyone in attendance so he could thank them. As he was going through the names in the guest book, he came across a name he wasn't sure of. He contacted a friend and asked about the name. Being reminded of who she was from the prayer fellowships, he sent her a message, thanking her for coming to the funeral. That's the kind of caring man Mickey was.

Over the next year, these two met occasionally over lunch. They talked of their families and their struggles in solo parenting. But mostly they were happy to have someone who understood the grieving process.

Like a neon sign from God, my friend felt she was supposed to introduce Mickey to me. She wasn't sure why God was nudging her in this direction. Was it to learn of my ministry to widows, since he helped lots of widows in his church? Was it for dating?

Meet someone? I thought. I had tried online dating sites. Because my qualifications were very specific, my luck on those sites had been only the bad kind. I did know that my qualifications for a second-chance relationship were far different from when I was a young adult. I had experienced some serious valleys in my marriage that changed some of my ideas for a future relationship.

My late husband had struggled with a secret addiction, so I had major trust issues. I had children at home, so I was still in the active parenting role, which meant I had control issues. I was middle-aged, so I was stubbornly set in my ways. I had been the boss in my house for over five years. Was I ready to give that up?

The online profiles were not lining up with my ideas. More importantly, I did not feel they were lining up with the kind of man God would want me with. I was unsure if God was leading me to become married again, or if I was the one trying to fill the void in my life. The online profiles I encountered claimed to be Christian, but when asked, they couldn't tell me anything about their faith. Some were not involved in a local church or rarely attended. Apparently finding someone online was far more difficult for me than advertised. I clearly needed someone with more hands-on potential than a possible match I found in Sweden.

At the suggestion of my friend, I took a risk in meeting Mickey. We shared our stories of love and loss. We shared pictures of our children and had a pleasant time together. After agreeing to meet again in a couple of days, we headed to our vehicles—I to my minivan and he to his big ol' country pickup.

We met a couple of days later for lunch. I allowed my heart to cautiously consider it as a date. *Great, he's prompt,* I thought, as we pulled up at the same time. Barely touching the chips and queso, we hardly paused in our three-hour chat. I was pleasantly surprised to see Mickey acting respectively toward the servers. We discussed the disappointments of our pasts and the way God had directed our lives through them.

When the topic of my late husband's addiction came up, he assured me that he never touched the stuff.

Well, God, now let's see where this leads. My heart began to unlock ever so slightly.

As we walked to the parking lot, I said, "I told my kids this was a date."

"Do you want it to be?"

"Yes, I think so."

For the next few days, I did some serious soul-searching. Was I ready for a relationship? Had God dropped this man in front of me? Was it possible to find someone near my age, who would help me parent my children? Could I help him raise his children? Where would we live? He had never lived in the city and I had always lived in the city. What church would we attend?

Our families were invested in our own churches, across town from each other. He taught children's Sunday school, and I worked in the baby nursery with my elderly mother. He drove a tractor on his acres, and I had neighbors I could talk to over the fence. He loved fishing, and I had never touched a fish. He played the radio, while I played piano and flute. I had more instruments than children, and he had more children than instruments.

God, I have been crushed so severely. How do I trust again? God had a lot of details to work out, and I was excited to see how He would do it. I decided to go along for the ride and risk opening my heart.

I threw him "curve balls" to see if he would stick around. I sent him my written testimony, sure that he would think I was just too much to handle.

Several times he said, joking, "Is that all you got?" He was confident God had caused our paths to cross.

We were at the mall, looking at suits one day, when two young men kept staring at us. *Did I teach them in school? Do I know them from church? Are they waiting to rob us?* I was suspicious as their eyes followed us throughout the store. We finished shopping and walked out into the mall.

The two men were waiting for us. "May we pray with you two?"

"Who are you praying to?" we asked.

After some questions about their faith, we finally allowed them to pray. In all my years of shopping, this had never happened before. The prayer had me weeping. Their words were exactly what we needed to hear. I know God had those young men at that spot to pray a blessing over us.

Since we only had a small window of opportunity between summer activities and fall school schedules, we went forward with wedding plans. Mickey's pastor agreed to officiate the wedding and wanted us to meet for counseling. We met over lunch with the pastor to discuss the shocking results of our compatibility test.

"In all my years of counseling, I have never had this happen," the pastor said.

I mentally began to grab my purse and leave the lunch, imagining the results.

"I have never had two people score more compatible," he said.

Did my ears deceive me? How could this be? But yes, our test revealed high compatibility in what really mattered, even as we were very different in how we lived. This once again was confirmation from our heavenly Father.

We had both been through the deepest valleys and had clung to our Savior through it all. Raising our children as solo parents made us both independent. We were not getting married because we needed someone. We *wanted* this person. We had depended on God and thrived during our deepest hurts.

All the details came together for the wedding. As I came down the aisle, escorted by my oldest son, one of my sons sang with his guitar. Most of our ten children joined us on stage during the ceremony as we prayed together for the blending of our families. The church was packed with family and friends from all over the state.

The pastor's remarks surprised me. His words lined up perfectly with the Hebrew words I had engraved on a ring I wore. Years earlier, I had chosen a ring to represent my following Christ, and now those words were in the wedding vows as I followed Mickey as he followed God. Another confirmation that God had been in the restoration business long before I even had a clue.

There had been so many times our "universes" ran parallel. Could God have been orchestrating our lives in a way that we would meet on that day in March? When we both had been praying for healing in our previous marriages, was it possible that God knew, even though healing on Earth wouldn't come, complete healing in Heaven would? We would have each other to heal from our grieving. Were we able to accept that our past relationships had prepared us for the current relationship?

God, through our deepest sufferings, brings our biggest restoration—in His timing, not ours. "And the God of all grace, Who called you to His eternal glory in Christ, after you have suffered a little while, will Himself restore you and make you strong, firm, and steadfast. To Him be the power for ever and ever. Amen" (1 Peter 5:10–11).

I could not have made up this story. As Mickey and I lived through our suffering by pointing to God's glory and never our own, God's power restored us. And our restoration includes each other.

It seems cliché to talk about our lives as a tapestry, but it describes life so well. We have beautiful colors of thread, but we have knotted and dark-colored ones too. Perhaps all our tapestries are woven together at certain times so God can show His restoration power.

We took a chance and said yes. He could have just as easily said, "No, she's a hot mess with too many kids. And besides, I'm never going to move to the city." Or I could have said, "He isn't perfect. I'm going to wait right here for someone perfect."

Sometimes God's restoration brings new ideas to make it clear that this was all from Him. We learned to walk through the suffering, clinging to the hand of God through His power. My suffering began with addiction and continued through widowhood, solo parenting, and downsizing our home. Mickey's suffering walked him through the ups and downs of taking care of an ill spouse for years and through adoptions, foster care, and job loss. When our faith was tested, God saw our faithfulness in following Him. It is only through God's strength that we survived.

We have led several sessions of GriefShare, where sharing our story has blessed so many others. We pointed others to the

Kingdom in a way we couldn't have done individually. We are a living testimony of God restoring beauty from ashes. And the beauty is all pointing to the Creator God.

I continue to write and speak with the online ministry to widows. So many widows want to understand how to fall in love for a second time, recognize the pitfalls, and experience amazing blessings. God has allowed me opportunities to share our story of blending families with all their ups and downs. I have learned to appreciate my gift of a spouse in a way I never had before. We have a full grasp on the fact that we aren't perfect, but we are perfectly imperfect for each other. Our faith has been tested beyond what we could have imagined, and our strength never came from our own willpower.

When God is all you have, you find He is all you need.

Elizabeth Dyer Covard is a remarried widow to Mickey. They both experienced the loss of their spouses and love to share the miracle of second chances. Their blended family includes ten children from middle school to adult. They homeschool the three youngest children and facilitate grief classes together. Through all the issues with blending, adoption, and widowhood, they are drawn closer to Christ. Psalm 94:19 has been a special verse for her family from the days her father was in VietNam through her new life with Mickey. Elizabeth writes and speaks with A Widow's Might, Inc., has published several devotionals, and leads conferences.

Thoughts to Ponder
from Suffering to Restoration

1. God works in unexpected ways.

2. Sometimes God brings new ideas to reveal His wisdom.

3. Out of your deepest suffering comes your greatest restoration story.

What has God restored in your life?

When anxiety was great within me,
your consolation brought me joy. — Psalm 94:19

Wins, Losses, and Firsts
by Joyce Brown

Maybe this would be my year! I tried to appear calm and confident, but my heart was pounding with anticipation. After competing in the pageant, I was standing on stage awaiting the results. Because I had covered every detail, I felt good about my performance.

Every morning at 6:30, I practiced the talent endlessly until I was exhausted. I worked out with my trainers four to five times a week, so my body was strong and defined. I hired an interview coach and learned who I am so I could confidently answer all the pageant questions. I purchased a beautiful pageant gown that accentuated my body and gave me confidence. The topping on the cake was my hair and makeup. Everything, including my performance, turned out exactly how I envisioned it. Perfect!

As I stood there, I was certain the results would be different from the year before, when I did not place or win. I knew I had competed with a strong performance that would result in me being named in the top four.

As the names were called, I glanced at one of the judges, who smiled at me—another good indication of the outcome. When the final name was called, I was still standing in the same spot. I had not placed . . . again. My ego was deflated. I was confused. *How could this happen again?*

After the pageant the year before, I reviewed my scores, then focused on making significant improvements in the areas where I scored the lowest. My prayer in everything I did was always, *God, You know I want this. However, if there are obstacles that will prevent me from being successful, or if I need more growth, please don't give it to me. You know what's best for me.* When I did not win the year before, I knew there were opportunities for improvement. I had stepped outside my comfort zone and tried something I had never done before. I was disappointed, but I thanked God for the opportunity.

This year was different—I had a stern talk with God. I felt I had done everything He led me to do, but the outcome was the same. Unbelievable. My discussion this year was, *God, I am not sure what happened, but You have some explaining to do.*

I graciously smiled and sincerely congratulated the winners. In my opinion, they had competed just like me. I had no animosity toward any of them. The judges apparently felt the other competitors were stronger and more in line with what the pageant represented.

I was disappointed in myself. How could I seriously think I could compete for such a prestigious title and represent the entire state of Texas? I had no pageant experience. My only experience was watching pageants on TV as a child. I thought pageants were glamorous and the women beautiful. I was a shy, quiet kid who tried not to be noticed, so pageants were not in my forecast. I did not know anyone in a pageant who could offer guidance. On my own, I tried my best to learn by researching the internet, purchasing a "How to Win a Pageant" CD, hiring a choreographer, pageant coach, makeup artist, and hairstylist. I had wasted all this money . . . again.

As I left the stage, I tried to be positive and cheerful. I accepted the results, but wondered if I would compete again. Probably not. I was extremely disappointed in myself. Friends and strangers told me I had done an excellent job. That positive feedback made me feel better. At least I had not made a fool of myself. I was not looking forward to seeing my family. They expected me to win, and minimally, that I would be a runner up. Neither happened. Despite their disappointment, I was not looking forward to seeing them put their best face forward. Like the year before, their comments would be positive, even though they knew I was as disappointed as they were.

While mingling in the crowd, someone tapped my shoulder and asked if I was Joyce Brown. When I said yes, I was told they immediately needed me backstage in the dressing room. Confused, I headed for the dressing room with a million thoughts racing through my head. This had not happened the year before.

When I entered the dressing room, all the other contestants and pageant board members were there. The room was in pandemonium with everyone asking what was going on. The contestants were asked to make a circle, and the director said that before beginning, we needed a word of prayer. After the prayer, the director said that a mistake had been made. The judge's votes were tallied incorrectly, resulting in incorrect winners being announced. The contestants were shocked and asked questions about how this could have happened. Still too early to confirm the outcome, we were told to stay in the room until the scores could be tallied again. Then more information would be available. I call this a "Steve Harvey" moment, because it was like the 2015 Miss Universe Pageant when he announced the wrong queen to be crowned.

Many of us had not seen our family before being ordered into the dressing room. We texted our families to inform them what was happening and tell them we could not come out until the correct results were announced.

While in the room, the director and board members apologized for the error. Of course, it was not intentional. They sent a strong message about the importance of getting the results right. They were transparent in their feedback and took total responsibility for the error.

When I registered to be a contestant, I did not know what to expect. I was not sure if the pageant would occur in a school auditorium or somewhere equivalent. Boy, was I wrong. I was impressed with the events leading up to the pageant. More impressive was the quality of the contestants, previous winners, and board members. All were warm and friendly. The effort that went into planning the pageant was beyond anything I could have imagined. The pageant board spared no expenses in finding the perfect high-end hotel to host the event. All the contestants felt like we were a part of something bigger than us and that we were important and specially selected. They did everything in their power to ensure the four-day affair was special. And it was.

I felt bad that the error happened despite their planning. However, for many years while working in a high technology company, I knew firsthand that unexpected errors occur, regardless of your best efforts to avoid them.

The woman who was announced as the queen had received her crown, sash, and roses. Like all queens, she completed her pageant walk across the stage to an audience of over 700 people. As the Royal Court was announced, they moved to the front of the stage. Afterward, they took pictures and greeted the crowd as winners of the pageant. *Now, if any of them were incorrect, how would this be corrected? How would the Royal Court react? Would they have to give up their roses and awards?* I felt overwhelmed, since I had so many unanswered questions.

While we waited for the correct results, the attitude in the room was incredibly positive and spiritual. We were all pulling for one another. In my opinion, a stronger bond of sisterhood was created because of this error. Words of encouragement were given to the ladies in the room, especially the queen and those holding their roses and awards.

Finally, after what felt like a lifetime, the director entered the room to announce the winners and explain how the error occurred. A new system had been implemented for tallying the results, as well as a new group of officials who did not completely understand the new system. It was the perfect storm. The results were tallied. She was now ready to announce the correct winners. I felt my mind and body go numb. It was my way of protecting myself from another disappointment. Although I heard the names being called, I did not comprehend any of it. Finally, she announced the winner of this year's pageant. She said the winner is . . . Joyce Brown.

I did not understand what happened until the woman who was named queen on stage raced over to me, handing me her flowers, sash, and crown. I burst into tears. Although I was extremely happy to win, the tears were because I empathized with her. She had taken her walk on stage and now felt disappointed, knowing that someone else had really won. It broke my heart.

The crowned queen, who was announced on stage was humble and gracious. We had met earlier at the pageant tea. During the pageant, we talked several times, and she told me three or four times that I was going to win. Although I thanked her, I was not as confident. I told her there were so many talented women in the pageant and everyone had the potential to win. After my name was called in the dressing room, she raced over to me and with a huge smile on her face said, "I told you, you were going to win." Through my tears, I apologized for what had occurred to her.

When I was crowned, the pageant was over, and most of the audience was long gone. The exception was the contestants' families and close friends, who were waiting to learn the outcome. The stage was torn down, and all the chairs in the auditorium were put away. I laughed and said, "I was crowned in the dressing room, sitting in a folding chair with only the contestants and the pageant board members—about thirty-five people." I took my queen's walk in the dressing room between the folding chairs while the contestants and I sang, "The Yellow Rose of Texas." Afterward, the contestants and board members graciously congratulated me. Many of them were equally disappointed that I was not crowned on stage. My response was, "God doesn't make mistakes." I believe everything happens for a reason. My daughter later said that it makes my story more compelling. I agree.

A board member told me to go across the hall to take pictures and took my hand to lead me to the other room. When I stepped out of the dressing room, my family and friends spotted me, ran toward me, and cheered hysterically. I was shocked. *Who told them I won?* Again, I burst into tears. This time they were sincere tears of joy. Witnessing the pride and joy my family experienced was overwhelming. I loved it. They witnessed the commitment, hard work, and dedication I had put into this challenge. Their words of encouragement meant the world to me. I had accomplished something bigger than me. My family supported me from the beginning. They never doubted my ability to win. I wanted to set the example for my girls and grandkids that anything is possible if you listen to God's voice, have faith, and know in your spirit that nothing is too big for God.

Later that night, I had a different conversation with God. I thanked Him with all my heart for such a tremendous opportunity. I thanked Him for allowing me to win the pageant and asked Him to guide me through this journey. I never want to walk alone. I need Him now more than ever. I also apologized for doubting His goodness and faithfulness. I am sure He heard me, because He continues to bless me.

The results gave me a sense of joy and relief. My hard work had paid off after all. My thoughts of inadequacy were replaced with the thought that I am good enough. After winning, I realized that God has a sense of humor. I thought I would win on a stage with everyone watching. God had something else planned. God proved once again that when I rely on Him, He is faithful and will always answer my prayers.

After I was crowned queen, my life profoundly changed. I did not know what to expect—it was new territory. I was given more opportunities than I could ever imagine. I met two politicians who presented me with resolutions. One resolution named Denton County in my honor for February 2020. I was asked to emcee a Senior Health Fair for a congresswoman. Many newspapers, television shows, and radio shows interviewed me. I participated in numerous parades, attended senior living events, and performed at many senior centers. I was also featured on a magazine cover and was a motivational speaker for several groups. Now, I am an author.

As a young girl and watching pageants on television, it is unbelievable that the quiet, shy girl who did not want to be noticed could blossom into such an amazing woman where all things are possible through God. All things are possible when we let His light shine through us.

Winning the pageant is a first for me. However, there have been many firsts. I was born the sixth of eight kids. Our parents did not complete high school, but they expected it from us. Higher education was not expected, since there was no money. After working in a factory for a year, I knew life had more to offer. I enrolled in college and was the first in my family to graduate. I had no role model but became a role model for my nieces and nephews. Not only had I completed college, but I received a Bachelor of Science in Electrical Engineering Technology in 1981, a time when not many women were getting technology degrees. After working as an engineer in a high technology company for five years, I landed my first supervisor job. As a woman of color, I had no role model. I became a role model and began mentoring other young women and engineers. I retired after a thirty-year career in corporate America in middle management.

God has been ever-present in my life, guiding me and opening doors. He has also been there creating challenges and putting obstacles in my path. God has known what I need to grow in my character and in Him. There have been many times that I have taken on challenges and wanted to quit. But God said no, so I kept going. I learned to trust God and knew all my challenges were working for my good, even though I did not like the pain and stress. In the end, it was worth all the challenges. I know who I am and Whose I am. I trust God with all my heart and would not change any of my life experiences. I am so glad I did not give up on God and have continued to walk with Him. I ask God, what is next? I know He has something exciting. I cannot wait.

Joyce Brown is a motivational speaker whose goal is to empower and motivate others to live their best life and pursue their goals regardless of age. She is the reigning 2019 Ms. Texas Senior America. At the age of 59, she lost fifty pounds by changing her eating habits and attending boot camp, and is now in the best shape of her life. Joyce received an Electrical Engineering Technology degree in 1981 and retired from corporate America after 38 years of service. She is also a certified health coach. Contact Joyce at 972-400-7045 or JoyceMTSA19@gmail.com.

Thoughts to Ponder
from Wins, Losses, and Firsts

1. Stop doing things in your finite strength and rely on God.

2. Cry out to God when you are hurting.

3. Your identity comes from God, not your efforts.

**What life goals
do you need to surrender to God?**

---

*In all these things we are more than conquerors
through Him who loved us. — Romans 8:37*

Searching for Home

by Vivien Chambers

My heels tapped click, click, click. *There's no place like home. There's no place like home.* I wasn't Dorothy from *The Wizard of Oz* and I had no ruby slippers, but that didn't stop me from trying to find my way home.

When I was six, my mom took my two older brothers and me to stay with her mom and brother. We left Memphis, Tennessee, to live in Arizona. I loved my grandmother and my quiet, loving uncle. However, I missed my dad. Mom was vague about when we'd go home. Dad called on Christmas Day to say Merry Christmas. "Your mom and I are getting a divorce," he said. "Enjoy your toys." Toys! We were too crushed to care about toys.

Dad remarried as soon as the divorce was final. When my brothers and I went to visit the following summer, he greeted us with his new wife, who had an adorable eighteen-month-old daughter. Dad and my brothers doted on my baby stepsister, Misty. I was jealous. I felt betrayed. Mom had been replaced, and so had I.

My brothers and I made frequent trips back and forth between parents. Shortly after our first return to Dad, he and my stepmom searched for a new home. They dropped Misty and me off to stay with her grandparents. I felt abandoned. I didn't know these people. The grandmother was grumpy, not pleased about having two kids dumped on her for a week. At least the grandfather was jovial and happy about our stay. Oh, he was delighted—like a spider with a fly in its web. The man liked little girls. He didn't molest Misty. I can't say the same for me. I was seven years old.

Dad was a contractor and relocated to Texas, then to different states in the north and the southeast. When a relationship or another marriage failed, Mom moved from Arizona and then to different cities in the west. We once moved five times in one year. By the time I was eleven, I had lived in nine different states—a few of them twice. I was almost always grieving. I missed whichever parent my brothers and I just left. I missed my grandmother and uncle and what few friends I made along the way. I desperately wanted a stable home life.

My oldest and favorite brother, Bob, was four years older than me. Alan was sixteen months older. We had a brutal pecking order. Bob picked on Alan, who in turn picked on me. These conflicts were physical, ending with the younger sibling hurt and crying. This made me tough. None of us picked on Misty. She was my rival for Dad's affection and five years younger, so I didn't play with her much. As a result, I was often lonely. I learned to enjoy playing alone and eventually preferred it.

School schedules were disrupted with no regard to how it affected our education. Yet we were expected to excel. I barely managed to make passing grades. I felt especially stupid when Dad told me tutoring was useless, because I couldn't grasp basic math concepts.

Dad was extremely strict about obedience, behavior, and manners. We were all well-acquainted with his belt, but his actions became more formidable when I was nine. He became verbally abusive, ridiculing and shaming my brothers and me. I was terrified as he stomped the spokes out of both my brothers' bikes after they fought over one because the other bike had a flat tire. This is the parent who took us to church regularly. He once beat Alan and me for giggling in church. Hard thumps behind the ear briefly stymied us, but one look at the other and we'd snicker again. Bob counted the swats. Even though I got less, the swats numbered in the teens.

I felt unloved and angry. We were told not to cry but were beaten on bare flesh until we did. The punishment was extreme for each minor offense. Dad never apologized for anything. The way I made him pay was to promise myself, the next time I lived with Mom, I would never return to Dad. I kept that promise.

The following summer, Mom and Grandma came to visit. My brother Alan and I were allowed to go with them when they left. We never looked back. Returning to Arizona was like going home, but it was bittersweet. Even though my brother Bob wanted to join us, he knew Mom's financial struggles and declined. I missed him. I also missed my beloved uncle, who died earlier that year. He was the kindest man I had ever known.

I thought I'd never stop crying when he died.

While I was living in Arizona at age ten, Mom's aunt and uncle visited. Like Misty's grandfather, this old man also liked touching little girls where he shouldn't. I was in my late teens when I finally told Mom about both incidents of sexual abuse. She casually mentioned that her uncle had assaulted her when she was young. I was speechless—appalled that she knew what this man was like and did nothing to protect me. Mom's admission cut deep. I felt betrayed and insignificant.

Fifth grade was the first time I completed a whole year at one school. However, that summer Mom married a man a week after they met and a month later moved the three of us to Washington state. Shortly afterward, she filed for divorce. We lived in Tacoma for the next ten years but kept moving to different school districts until I was in the seventh grade.

Mom met a man with two young sons, who lived with us off and on until they married. He was a pitiful alcoholic with a vulgar mouth. He was never harsh with any of us kids, nor did he crack innuendos about me. He and Mom divorced soon after I graduated from high school.

For my entire childhood, I was at the mercy of my parents' whims. Adults could do whatever they wanted, and we kids had to go along, regardless of how we felt or how it affected us. My mind told me that my parents loved me. My heart, however, wasn't so sure.

We sang, "Jesus loves me, this I know," in Sunday school, but love was ambiguous. I tried to be good but didn't know how. What little I did know, I couldn't do. There's a chapter in the Bible that talks about continually doing things you don't want to do and then not doing the good things you want to do. That was me. I wanted to please God but was too weak. Exposure to sexuality at an early age seemed impossible to overcome. Even so, none of this prevented me from being religious. I went to church faithfully.

Family dysfunction hindered me from developing healthy social skills. Respect for my elders was pounded into me. Needless to say, I seriously lacked personal boundaries.

I started dating my first boyfriend at fourteen. He was funny, loving, and patient when I was obnoxious. His only hang-up was he wanted sex. I managed to resist for over a year by breaking up with him. Doing this made me feel lost and lonely. So we'd get back together and break up again until I eventually stopped resisting. Then I got pregnant.

Part of me savored the idea of a baby of my own to love. However, I was afraid and too young and immature to raise a child, not to mention provide for one. Mom offered to help, but I didn't want to bring a baby into our messed-up family. My biggest fear was losing friendships when those at church discovered my hypocrisy. A month before my sixteenth birthday, I had an abortion. I despised my weakness and selfishness. I deliberately hardened my heart to numb the pain. That didn't work any better than clicking my heels for home.

Although I continued to go to church regularly for the next two years, I wandered farther from the God I didn't know. I severed ties with my boyfriend and found it harder to resist other guys I dated. At eighteen, just out of high school with no job and nowhere to go, I took a live-in nanny position for an eight-year-old girl whose father was a long-haul truck driver. He was twenty-six and divorced. Within a month, I gave up my losing battle for sexual abstinence. With the hope of marriage, I moved from my room into his. I stopped going to church with friends across town and didn't consider going to the small church at the end of our street.

My boss-turned-boyfriend introduced me to marijuana for occasional recreation. After a while, a neighbor and I started smoking pot daily. This didn't help my mood. Living with someone who was gone most of the time made me sad and lonely. My longing for love was so insatiable that I grew jealous of the precious father-daughter relationship and the time they spent together. I became depressed and started withdrawing. I missed being around Christians. More than that, I wanted God in my life. After two-and-a-half years, I cried and prayed in desperation, "God, if You'll get me out of this mess, I'll serve You for the rest of my life." Within a month, I started receiving grant money to take an eighteen-month course at a vocational school. The first check went to essentials. The second went to rent an apartment.

I didn't go to church right away. I wasted the first year of school on a brief relationship and smoking pot. The first summer, I befriended a neighbor who invited me to church. She went to the very church where I had moved from. It didn't take long to get bored with services. I fought to stay awake through sermons. My attendance waned. One Sunday I found myself thinking, *Sing and pray, pray and sing. If Heaven is anything like this, I'm not so sure I want to go.* Then I got a *New King James* Bible for Christmas. Reading in modern language made it understandable and relevant.

A young preacher from Seattle was invited to our church to teach a Wednesday night class on the life of Christ. He and a group from Texas started a campus ministry at the University of Washington. The ministry offered weekend retreats, called Campus Advance, three times a year for college students and young adults. One weekend, our class was invited to an Advance retreat. A few of us went.

The January retreat was held in the Cascade Mountains, quilted with patches of snow. The contrast between the frigid darkness outside and the warm, brightly lit lodge was not lost. What I witnessed inside stopped me in my tracks. About fifteen to twenty smiling young adults stood in rows, enthusiastically singing worship songs. Across each row, people held hands, or arms were draped over shoulders or around waists of those on the right and left, regardless of gender. This was new to me, especially among religious people. These people seemed to love one another.

That Saturday night, someone read a detailed medical account of what Jesus endured the night He was crucified. I knew Jesus died on the cross to wash away all my wrongs, and it made me sad. I preferred to think of His resurrection without pausing to reflect on the depth of His suffering.

I heard that Jesus was beaten, and His beard hair was yanked out. The thorns fashioned into a crown weren't short like those found on rose bushes. They were an inch-long, thick, very sharp, and cut deeply into Jesus' forehead and scalp as the crown was shoved onto His head. The whip used to beat Him had several long tails tied with sharp barbs of metal and pottery on each end. This didn't leave whelps and bruises like the lashes Dad gave me for giggling in church. The scourging Jesus received wrenched flesh off His entire torso. By the thirty-ninth stroke, His flesh was lacerated and stripped to the bone. He was forced to carry a heavy crossbeam until He became too weak. On the cross, the weight of His body was supported by six-inch spikes driven through His wrists and feet.

Crucifixion was not a quick death. It was so painful that no word previously existed to accurately describe it. The derivative of the crucifixion is excruciation. Jesus lived for hours on the cross. He had to push His shredded back up rough wood to stand on His nail-pierced feet to breathe. He didn't bleed to death. His lungs filled with fluid, and He suffocated as soon as He stopped pushing to stand.

Though I fully understood Jesus' anguish, even today I can't fathom the extent of such pain. I can, however, relate to a fraction of His emotional anguish.

I felt betrayed. Jesus was betrayed with the kiss of a friend who handed Him over to those who tortured and killed Him.

I felt unloved. Jesus was despised and rejected by His own people.

I felt used, unimportant, unaccepted, and alone. People who once hailed Jesus as a king turned against Him and demanded His death. Even His closest friends scattered at His arrest.

I was filled with shame. Jesus was stripped naked and hung on public display.

My father hurt me. Some of Jesus' final words were, "My God, My God, why have You forsaken Me?"

Jesus suffered far more than I ever did. The major difference is He suffered willingly. He did it for love. And He did it for me. I deserved punishment for all the hateful, self-centered, shameful things that separated me from God. Jesus came to Earth to take my punishment so I could join Him in Heaven.

Like seagulls flying along the Washington state waterfront, foraging and begging for scraps and handouts from passersby, I scrounged for love. And like the greedy gull accustomed to being fed or denied, I became demanding. I came to the Advance retreat like a gull saturated from an ocean oil spill. I was heavily weighed down by childhood abuse, neglect, legalism, and most of all, by my own bad choices. Jesus lifted me up, washed me off, and released me to fly. And fly, I did. I soared straight home to the flock who awaited me.

The few friends who attended the Advance retreat agreed—we needed to take the love of Jesus to our home church. We started among our peers with weekly Bible studies. We introduced new songs to the church and stood together holding hands or draping arms over shoulders, singing with enthusiasm and joy. Sermons became meaningful. Instead of dozing, I diligently took notes. Our love and enthusiasm spread to senior members. The whole church was transformed and filled with joy and love.

I moved to Texas after getting married and heard from a friend, twenty-five years later, that the church was still going strong. So am I.

A lost and lonely girl ascended that cold, dark mountain to the Advance retreat. A beloved child—adopted into the family of God, descended. Although I'm not home yet, my heavenly Father is preparing a place for me. The welcome I'll receive upon arrival will be greater than my first Advance retreat.

Guess what. No matter what you've experienced; no matter what you've done, or how you feel about yourself, Jesus knows. He understands and He cares. His suffering wasn't for me only. It was for you too. He invites you to accept His love and forgiveness. I pray you will.

My home is in Heaven, where there is no place like home. As Mr. Rogers used to say, "Won't you be my neighbor?"

Vivien Chambers was born in Champaign, Illinois, and lived in several states before spending her latter childhood years in Tacoma, Washington. She moved with her husband to Texas where they've remained since 1981. She has served as a Stephen Minister and presently enjoys volunteering as an assistant in a Multiple Sclerosis water aerobics class. She and her husband of forty years have five grown children and six grandchildren.

Thoughts to Ponder

from Searching for Home

1. God understands your emotions.

2. Christ suffered a brutal death so you can have eternal life.

3. Your permanent home is in Heaven with Jesus.

When have you seen someone demonstrate Christ's love?

We know that if the earthly tent we live in is destroyed, we have a building from God, an eternal house in Heaven, not built by human hands. — 2 Corinthians 5:1

Twenty-Seven Hours of Agony
by Melinda Propes

What is the worst thing that you can imagine happening in your life? Maybe you have already experienced that, or maybe you don't even want to think of what that might be. I've experienced great loss. I lost my mom to cancer and survived a traumatic house fire. But the worst thing I can imagine is losing my husband or one of my children, their spouses, or my grandchildren. The circle of ones I love continues to grow. When you love someone, you are at risk of being deeply hurt.

In September of 1998, my son Jeff began his tenth-grade school year. Our daughter, Emily, had flown the nest and was away at college. Things seemed quite different around our house, and we were still adjusting to our new normal. One day Jeff walked in and handed me his packet of school photos, taken a few weeks earlier. While admiring his handsome photo, I noticed a rather odd lump on the side of his neck. I turned to look at him and sure enough, there it was, subtle but definitely present. With no obvious cause, we decided to watch it for a little while, assuming it would go away.

Two weeks later, the lump was still there. Much to my fifteen-year-old's dismay, I made an appointment to see our trusted family pediatrician. Off we went, my nearly six-foot-tall son with the budding football player physique, to the waiting room of our pediatrician's office. The visit was routine, but the doctor was puzzled at the cause of the lump. Jeff was given a round of antibiotics to clear up any possible infection. The doctor instructed us to return after two weeks for follow-up.

When the two-week waiting period was over, we went back to the doctor. The antibiotics had not helped. The doctor talked about surgery and suggested the name of a specialist, because the lump would probably have to be surgically removed. Finally, as we left, he sent us to the hospital for a chest x-ray, which seemed a little odd, but I trusted the doctor completely.

Sometimes, ignorance is bliss. I obediently made the appointment with the recommended specialist and a short time later, we went to see the surgeon, still blissfully unaware of storm clouds building on the horizon. The pediatric surgeon was someone we'd seen before with an earlier health scare. There had been several in Jeff's past—the heart murmur scare, the brain tumor scare, unusual-looking moles that had to be removed, a variety of normal and sometimes not so normal childhood complaints.

This latest episode just seemed like one more in a long line of the unusual. An experienced parent learns to take such things in stride. All the other scares had turned out fine, and this one would too, or so I expected.

After a few moments, the surgeon brought in a colleague. Now there were two doctors, scratching their chins and nodding their heads together. They went into the hall, whispering, which is never a good sign. When our surgeon came back in, he announced that the lump must be removed immediately. He talked about surgery the following week, which seemed way too fast for me.

Whoa! Let's slow down a minute here. It was almost time for Jeff's fall break from school and that seemed a much better option than missing a day of school for such a surgery. I asked the doctor if we could wait for another two weeks until fall break, and he hesitantly agreed.

Jeff was not thrilled to be having surgery, and especially not during his fall break from school. To me, this whole thing was happening much too quickly, but I resolved to keep a good attitude and get on with it. It was just one more thing to add to the list of Jeff's weird medical history.

Two weeks later, we confidently drove to Children's Medical Center in Dallas, ready to get it over and behind us. Neither my husband nor I were worried because the doctor had explained the surgery, saying it would only take about an hour to an hour-and-a-half. It was my job to be the reassuring mother, and I tried to relay to Jeff that it would all be over soon and not to worry. After all, they were experts at Children's Medical Center, so Jeff was in good hands.

To pass the time during surgery, I tried to read a book, but nervous, restless energy kept me from focusing. Ken spent most of his time on his cell phone handling work calls. In what seemed like no time at all, the doctor returned to give us the post-surgery report. I should have immediately known from his manner that something was amiss, especially when he sat down and didn't look us in the eye.

"Surgery went well," he said, "and the tumor removed was quite large." Next, he said it was one of the largest of its type he had ever removed during his many years as a surgeon. *Wow!* And then the doctor said, "Your son has Hodgkin's Lymphoma, and you will need to plan on going to Houston to MD Anderson, right away for more tests. You'll probably start chemotherapy by the end of the week."

What? That's not possible. The doctor added, "Of course, all this is dependent on the results of the biopsy," which he had asked to be rushed through. He stressed again that he had seen a lot of tumors, and although we would have to wait on the official biopsy results, he was sure it was Hodgkin's. He said we should expect to hear back from him with the biopsy results the next day, but in the meantime, plan on going to Houston. We should know the results for sure within twenty-four hours. Again, unable to look us in the eye, the doctor walked out.

Time stopped and it felt like all the air had been sucked out of the room. I couldn't breathe. Ken was staring at the floor. What was there to say? We both sat stunned. Tears welled up in my eyes, and I wanted to burst out crying. But at that moment, the nurses wheeled my still groggy son back into the room, sitting in a wheelchair. The nurses explained he was waking up faster than expected, and they thought he would like to be with us. They told us to sit for a short while to be sure he was okay, and then we could go home.

At that moment, it was hard to know what to do, where to look, how to focus on anything other than the word "cancer." However, my groggy son sat there needing me, so I tried to pull myself together. There was no sense letting him see the fear in my eyes, so like the doctor, I kept looking away. Bless my husband at that moment. As he had already proven in the "great fire episode," he's really good in a crisis. He took over, making conversation with Jeff, and I got up to pace the room, trying desperately to pull myself together.

I remember turning around, hearing someone call my name. There in the doorway to the waiting room stood my good friend, Diana. I stepped into the hallway, quietly collapsing on her shoulder, as I struggled to tell her the bad news. We cried together.

"What are you doing here?" I asked.

"I'm not sure," she replied. "I just had to come."

Before the day of surgery, she volunteered to come along for moral support. But thinking the surgery would be no big deal and knowing Ken would be there, I declined her offer. When she unexpectedly showed up at the hospital and found me, she said she'd been praying for us that morning and could not reach peace in her spirit. There was a strong urging in her spirit that I needed her. Finally, not knowing why, she set off to find us. Having no idea where she could find us in such a big place, she drove to the hospital. When she walked in and continued walking, she ended up at our very door at just the right moment.

There are no words to express the gratitude I felt, knowing I had the support of my dear friend, in what was the worst moment of my life. No one will ever be able to convince me that God is not real. If I had any doubts, which I did not, they would all have been swept away at that moment. The God who rules the universe knew my need and sent my best friend to provide comfort and support. Having Diana near me did not change the bad news, but it reminded me that I was not alone. God knew what was going on, and He was right there in the midst of it. Whatever happened next, I knew I was not alone.

Although I have no memory of the trip home, we made it home from the hospital. Ken and I tried to keep our restless fifteen-year-old son quietly occupied for the rest of the day. The passing hours seemed to creep by. We had to make difficult phone calls to share the news. Friends and family wanted to know how the surgery went. I could barely say the word "cancer," but found myself crying on the phone with my mother, trying to explain what Hodgkin's disease was, even though I had little idea myself. Knowing I had few emotional resources left, I asked Mother to call my sister and brother and give them the news.

Ken talked to our good family friends in Houston, explaining Jeff's diagnosis. Apparently, we would see them sooner than expected. After all, MD Anderson was located where they lived.

48

The one call I couldn't make was to my daughter. I absolutely could not tell her that her brother might have cancer. Not wanting to rock her world that way, I reasoned that I could tell her after the biopsy results came in the next day before we headed south to Houston.

Since Ken needed to take time off work to get us to MD Anderson, he had his own plans to make. He spent time upstairs watching TV with Jeff, and I spent time in my bedroom, laying on my bed, crying and praying desperate prayers until I finally dropped off to sleep, utterly spent. I reached the end of myself. There was nothing left. It was up to God now.

Because the doctor said the biopsy results would be rushed through and to expect him to call within twenty-four hours, once the clock reached 1:00 pm the next day, my phone vigil began. Waiting on such life-changing news is not easy. *Tick-tock, tick-tock.* Time crept slowly by. Minute by minute, hour by hour, I tried to keep busy, staring at the clock. *Tick-tock, tick-tock.*

Entertaining my restless son helped a little. He still did not suspect anything was wrong, and I hoped to keep it that way. Somehow the day passed, and still, there was no phone call from the doctor. Finally, at 5:00 pm, my phone rang. I looked at the phone knowing it was the doctor, and for a split-second thought about not answering. Maybe not hearing the fateful words I expected to hear would make them not true. I could pretend just a little longer that everything was fine.

"Hello?"

The biopsy results were back, and everything looked clear. There was no cancer, the doctor said. Joy! Indescribable joy. Wonder. Amazement. Relief. Thank you, God.

It was a vastly different sounding doctor I now had on the phone, no longer somber, sounding almost lighthearted, making me realize that giving such bad news to parents must be a difficult part of his job. How grateful I felt in those brief moments, thanking him for calling and especially for the giving of such good news. The doctor ended by saying he wanted to see Jeff for a follow-up visit two weeks after surgery.

Now, there were many more phone calls to make to share our good news, a much easier thing than sharing bad, but it was still exhausting. Time passed and before long we were back in the surgeon's office for our follow-up visit. Everything was healing nicely, he said, and there was no need to return. It was over. Before we left, however, the doctor wanted to have a private conversation with me. Jeff was sent to the waiting room while I went with the doctor into his office.

He told me that in his more than twenty years as a surgeon, he had never removed a tumor so large. Having seen it so many times before, he was sure it was cancer. Clearly mystified, he had no explanation for the clear biopsy results. There was obvious puzzlement and a little bit of discomfort on his part. Before we finished our discussion, the doctor also shared other unexpected and frightening news.

During surgery, he discovered that the large tumor was spreading tentacles into the surrounding tissue of Jeff's neck and face. Had the surgery not happened when it did, the doctor said Jeff could have experienced permanent nerve damage in his face because of nerves being damaged or cut in the removal process. By asking to have surgery put off until fall break, I had put my son in jeopardy. The doctor and I spent a little more time discussing possible explanations for the start of the tumor, but there was no way to determine the cause. It would have to remain an unsolved mystery.

I have learned a few things since that horrible day at the hospital. Hodgkin's Lymphoma is cancer, but it is not necessarily fatal. Had the tumor been cancerous, it would have been a challenging journey for our family, and life would have changed drastically, maybe forever.

In the years since, Jeff thinks of the scar on his neck as a symbol, an ever-present reminder of how close he came to a life-changing event. It reminds him to be grateful for healing. Over the years, I have told this story to others and they invariably ask me what I think happened. Do I think the doctor was wrong after surgery? Did he make a mistake? Am I angry because he falsely told me such bad news?

More than one person has suggested that Jeff received miraculous healing. Do I believe healing miracles still happen today? To that question, I can answer yes. Why do some people receive healing miracles and others do not when we pray? Only God knows the answer to that one. As Christians, our job is simply to pray. Then in faith and trust, we must leave the outcome to God. Hard though, extremely hard.

Another lesson learned during those painful twenty-seven hours is that I could survive things I never dreamed possible. I saw and experienced the compassion of God and now know for certain that God is present with us during our pain, whatever the circumstances.

I am also grateful for how God used my friend, Diana. She does not like to drive to unfamiliar places and when possible, avoids freeways. That day, for me, she stepped out of her comfort zone to find me. She didn't know why she was going, only that she needed to go. She also didn't know where to park or how to find us in the hospital, but in blind faith, she walked to and arrived at the door of my waiting room. This all happened in less than ten minutes after I received the worst news of my life. Timing is everything, especially God's timing. To me, that is the truest miracle of that horrible day.

Thank God for sending my friend, and thank God my friend was listening and obedient when she felt the call to go. May we all be so sensitive and willing to go to the aid of someone in need when God wants to send us.

"Then I heard the voice of the Lord saying, 'Whom shall I send? And who will go for us?' And I said, 'Here am I. Send me!'" (Isaiah 6:8).

Melinda Propes is a new author who loves sharing inspirational faith stories. Earlier careers include working as a draftsman/technical illustrator, a psychologist's assistant, and owning and operating a longarm quilting business. Melinda enjoys traveling with her husband of forty-four years and spending time with her two children and their families. She believes in giving back to her community and regularly volunteers at her church, a local food pantry, and Bible Study Fellowship.

Thoughts to Ponder
from Twenty-Seven Hours of Agony

1. God goes before you in all things, preparing the way.

2. With God's help, you can endure much more than you ever thought possible.

3. When you feel prompted by the Holy Spirit, act without delay.

When have you felt prompted by the Holy Spirit?

I love the Lord, for He heard my voice;
He heard my cry for mercy. — Psalm 116:1

I Am the Woman at the Well

by Mayada Naami

After a failed engagement, two failed marriages, and nine lovers, I am like the woman at the well described in the Bible.

My journey began in Baghdad, Iraq, in 1969, the year of the Baghdad hangings. My mother was two months pregnant with me. On the horrific day of January 27, 1969, Baghdad radio invited citizens to Liberation Square to "enjoy the feast." Reportedly, more than 500,000 attended the hangings. People danced and celebrated before the corpses of the fourteen convicted spies (nine Jews, three Muslims, and two Christians). The three remaining Jews of the initial twelve were executed on August 26, 1969, the day I was born.

Fearing the State of Iraq, Saddam Hussein's growing popularity, and foreseeing the future of Iraq under Saddam's reign, my dad made the ultimate sacrifice to save his wife and young family. Stepping out in blind faith, he packed only a few suitcases so he would not arouse suspicion. He pretended his family was going on vacation to visit his wife's family in Beirut, Lebanon. In reality, he never planned to return. He left everything else behind and never looked back.

When we left Iraq, I was six months old. I celebrated my first birthday in Lebanon while we awaited our immigration visa to Canada. Moving to Canada and growing up in a strict Catholic Middle Eastern family in a western world was complex. Even though we were Catholic and my dad was raised in a predominantly Muslim country, he adopted the many strict attitudes and traditions regarding women and their role in the family. As a female, I was controlled with fear, guilt, and shame.

My dad took his obligation to "marry off" his five daughters seriously. Growing up, I was never allowed to make friends with non-Middle Easterners or have a boyfriend. So it was home, school, and church on Sundays until I was married off. Every Sunday, my mom made me don my Sunday best to be paraded in front of other church members. The hope was that one day I would be chosen as a wife. I did not understand this until I was almost sixteen years old. After that, I dreaded going to church on Sundays, knowing that I was being scrutinized by every person to whom I was introduced. It was less of a church and more of a "meat market."

Girls in their late teenage years were considered old enough to get married. I was engaged at the age of eighteen to a man whose aunt knew my mom. He was the only son of a wealthy Iraqi. Although his parents lived in Iraq, he was sent to Toronto in the early 1980s to avoid the wartime draft before he turned eighteen. We were engaged to be married, never dated, and only spent time together while chaperoned by my entire family. I thought something was not right, but I ignored my inner voice and went along with the family tradition.

On behalf of his parents, his aunt asked my mom for my hand in marriage. We were engaged by May, and during this time he showered me with lavish gifts. I thought he was so romantic, and I was falling in love. Every few weeks, he came to visit me with bags of expensive clothes, perfumes, and designer watches. As time went by, he told me to get my hair permed, because he liked curly hairy. He wanted me to eat more, because I was too skinny. Even though I was raised to be respectful of men in our culture, I questioned his motives for showering me with numerous gifts. My inner voice said, *This is not right.*

The night of our engagement party, he gave me a Swiss gold watch and left the receipt inside the gift bag. When I questioned why the receipt was in the bag, he replied that it was for insurance purposes. However, deep down he wanted me to know how much the watch cost. We argued before the reception. I told him I felt like I was a possession, a doll he was dressing up to parade around as his soon-to-be trophy wife. He got angry and told me that any other woman would have jumped up and thanked and hugged him for the watch. Something was wrong, but once again I ignored that inner voice.

Throughout the engagement party, he did not speak to me. I put on my happy face and acted like it was the happiest day of my life. After our engagement, he made decisions about our future without discussing them with me. When I questioned him, he became angry and did not speak to me for days. This continued for a few months. One day, he broke off the engagement. During the year after that breakup, I was hurt and confused. I did not understand why he broke off the engagement. I had given him my virginity and was ashamed.

My mother kept pushing me to go to church on Sundays, and I refused. I was back on the "market" but did not feel like being paraded in front of everyone. My mother was upset. She told me people were gossiping, and I must get over my fiancé. Otherwise, no other man would marry me. I finally gave in and went to church. That's how I met and married my first husband.

He was also a Middle Eastern man who grew up in Lebanon and moved to Canada as a teenager. The month before the wedding, my fiancé's family invited my parents to dinner. His parents wanted to postpone the wedding. My fiancé confronted his mother, and they argued fiercely. At the end of dinner, my mother fainted, and his two brothers, who were both doctors, helped revive her.

We left his parents' home, and my dad said the wedding was off. My fiancé left with us. He still wanted to marry me and walked away from his own family. I did not feel right about it. All the way home I thought, *This is wrong. We should not get married without his family's blessing.* When I shared these thoughts with my fiancé, he said we were going to get married, and he did not care if his family attended the wedding. It felt all wrong, but once again I ignored the voice in my head. In retrospect, I know the voice in my head, which I kept ignoring, was the Holy Spirit.

The marriage lasted thirteen years. We had two children, a boy and a girl. As my son grew up, he spoke to my daughter in the same manner that my husband spoke to my daughter and me. When I realized I was raising my son to think this controlling behavior was acceptable, I was compelled to leave. As a Catholic Middle Eastern girl, I felt I was bringing shame to my family by getting a divorce.

As soon as one of the men I worked with heard I was getting a divorce, he asked me out for a date. Within three months, I was married. I thought it would be less shameful to be married than divorced, and I did not want to be a single mother. He was not controlling, but we did not have the same family values. That marriage lasted seven years.

At the end of my second marriage, I questioned my family's beliefs and traditions. Since childhood, I believed in God but did not have a personal relationship with Him. My mother, a devout Catholic, prayed constantly. I witnessed small miracles every day. When I was young, my mother survived a rare vaginal cancer. Doctors had given her three months to live.

Today she is alive and well at seventy-nine years old. She outlived the doctors and their predictions. She has one functioning kidney and has survived breast cancer and diabetes. The power of prayer is unarguable after witnessing my mother's life. Her positivity and undying faith have been an undeniable factor in my belief that there is a God.

After a failed engagement and two failed marriages, I felt ashamed and afraid of my future as a twice-divorced woman in a culture that regarded divorce as a sin. I asked God why I was getting divorced again. He lovingly said, *I did not choose them for you. You let someone else or your circumstances choose you for them.* It was at that moment I finally understood why I had lived in shame, fear, and guilt and allowed these strongholds to control my life. The decisions I made or allowed others to make for me were not of the Holy Spirit.

I cried and cried. All the shame I had felt was cleansed from my soul. Then I told the Lord that I did not want to be married to a man. I wanted to be the bride of Christ. I was broken and humbled in spirit. I was sad, hurt, tired, and disappointed.

The next month, I lost my job. Six months later, the house went to foreclosure, and I filed for bankruptcy. I was now homeless. I prayed constantly, and my heart was filled with hope even though my life was falling apart.

Then my whole life changed.

It was Saturday before the Lent season when I talked to a friend about my troubles. She asked me what I was going to give up for Lent. At first, I thought about giving up meat, since that was the Catholic tradition. Instead, I told her I wanted to give up control of my life. I wanted to get in the passenger seat and let God be in the driver's seat.

She laughed and said that would be hard for someone like me. I did not think I was controlling. I was engaged and had been married to a controlling person. *How can she think I am controlling?* I was a perfectionist. I always tried to make things right. And I looked for ways to make things happen. But controlling? I was tired and didn't want to think about it anymore.

The next day, she asked where I was going to church. I told her I did not have a church home, so she invited me to her church. She had only attended twice since her husband passed away and wanted me to go with her. So I did.

The next morning, I sat in the pew next to my friend. The pastor started his sermon by saying, "I know this is going to sound sacrilegious. It's the Sunday before Lent, and some of you are going to give up meat. Others will give up chocolate or soda. I say do not give up any of that. Why don't you give up control? Let God be in the driver's seat, and you get in the passenger seat."

I looked at my friend and she looked at me in shock. I started crying. For the second time in nine months, I heard God speak to me. I had just said those exact words to my friend the day before.

For the first time, I realized I was deeply wounded by rejection and wanted to control every circumstance around me. This caused me to have a spirit of control. At that moment, I completely surrendered and was filled with the Holy Spirit. Even though I was born in a very controlling environment, riddled with shame, guilt, manipulation, and fear, I was reborn that day by the Holy Spirit and adopted by God.

Like the Samaritan woman at the well, described in John 4:39–42, we all feel rejected and shamed by society, but God loves us despite our bankrupt lives. God loves us enough to actively seek us, to welcome us to intimacy, and to rejoice in our worship.

Mayada Naami is a Christian woman who has dedicated her life to inspiring other women to break free from the strongholds of insecurity, rejection, fear, and shame, which are inflicted by the lies of the enemy. Born in Iraq and raised Catholic, Mayada currently lives in Dallas, Texas. She believes the truth changes your life and the only truth is Jesus Christ. Mayada knew of Jesus but did not know Him until she fell in love with Him when she was reborn in 2011. Since then, she lives in the peace that comes only from the True Source. Contact her at MayadaNaami@gmail.com.

Thoughts to Ponder

from I Am the Woman at the Well

1. Jesus' sacrifice means you do not have to be controlled by guilt and shame.

2. God actively seeks you.

3. God wants you to seek Him.

> ### *How might control hinder your surrender to God?*

There is now no condemnation for those who are in Christ Jesus. — Romans 8:1

Falling Off the Radar

by Jenni Eastin

Have you ever watched the news when a plane has reportedly gone missing? They show a visual representation of the course that the plane was traveling and the spot where the plane suddenly fell off the radar and cannot be seen anymore. It disappears off the map. No one can pick up the signal, detect the course ahead, or accurately calculate the probability that the plane will arrive at its destination.

No one can provide help or comfort to the family members who have passengers on that plane. Sometimes search and rescue efforts recover the plane and the people who boarded, and sometimes there is no recovery at all.

That was my greatest fear. Not of planes, but that I had fallen off God's radar. I was afraid that I was all alone, without direction, or without anyone to see or comfort me. My daddy traveled every week and was busy climbing the corporate ladder. My mother and I were disconnected. It seemed disloyal to talk about it. There was a big, empty, sad space in my life, and I needed to be heard, seen, and comforted. But there was no one there—or that is how it felt. From early on, I wondered who I could trust. I felt alone, misunderstood, and unseen—off everyone's radar.

I was five when I realized that my father was an alcoholic and I could do nothing to budge that. My parents buried a child who died in my mother's womb, and I watched my father drink, trying to numb his pain with overconsumption of alcohol. I desperately wanted to connect with him and be a source of his joy, but nothing I did made a difference. I wondered if there was a God who saw and knew the things I knew—things that were too embarrassing to talk about.

Every night was the same. The pouring of the drink, the puddling sound of alcohol hitting the glass, the clanking of the ice. I kept a close eye on all that was going on, but I felt helpless and unable to make a difference. It was like watching a plane that disappeared off the radar and being unable to help with the rescue efforts. I wished there was someone or something, a

Creator or a God, Who could transform the things that I could not change. I longed for someone to trust. I felt hopeless.

My mother began taking me to church, and the more I heard about God, the more I was encouraged to trust Him. Although my parents had done their best, trust was the one thing that I chose to reserve. I heard talk of having a relationship with God, and I wondered what that would look like and what that would mean.

Around the age of twelve, it became clear to me that there was no hope of things coming together or of anything in my life changing without the help of a great big God. I asked Him to show me that I could trust Him, and I surrendered my dream of having a sober father to a God I could not see or understand. There is a Bible verse where God asks us to call out to Him, and in response, He will tell us unsearchable things that we do not know. I decided to call out to God and believe what He said was true. I waited to see how God would work in this situation. I was desperate.

As I talked to God and asked Him to show me His plans for my life, I began to see things change in deep and powerful ways in my father's life. Although he never had any interest in learning or talking about God, he agreed to attend church with my mother and me. Ultimately, my father trusted God with his life too. Not only did he begin to have a personal relationship with God, but he surrendered his desire to be in charge and began to lean on God to help him as he made decisions in business and for our family. Not only was my father going to church, but he was volunteering to help at church and became a regular usher. Although he was not comfortable at first, he prayed at family meals. He wanted to learn what the Bible says, know God, and follow His principles.

As I watched the way God worked things out, I became more optimistic when I saw how God kindly answered my father's prayers and changed his heart. I felt secure that God was in control. Ultimately, God led my father down a path of freedom and sobriety.

There was another time when I felt like I fell off the radar in life. Even before I got married, I trusted God that someday I would have children. Although I believed God had a plan for my husband and me to have a family, I had no idea what that would look like. At the age of thirty-one, I was unable to get pregnant. The doctors told me I would not be able to have children on my own, and the infertility specialists were unsure that they could help me. I was devastated. I sank in my seat and felt completely inadequate as a woman. I resented anyone who could get pregnant on her own. The only time I got pregnant and got a "yes" on the pregnancy test, I miscarried. I lost that baby at six weeks, which left me feeling more confused, empty, and unseen—like I had crashed and was no longer visible on the map.

Amid my pain, I discovered that God did see me and was a wonderful friend. He encouraged me through His words in the Bible on difficult days. People came into my life at specific times, who seemed to be an extension of God's love. I needed guidance and discernment to get me back on course.

On days when I lacked direction, God sent someone from His unofficial search and rescue team to encourage me. I felt increasingly able to trust that God could see me and that He had a plan. Although it was not easy, knowing God made things bearable. One day stands out in my mind. I had just visited the doctor, and my body was not responding well to the in-vitro medicine. The results were unimpressive. After all of the dedication and financial expenses that had been forfeited, my reproductive system was failing, and there was talk about canceling my in-vitro cycle altogether. I left the doctor's office, slumped down in the seat of my car, and began talking to the Lord. I told Him how disappointed I was, and I asked Him to send extra comfort and encouragement. I needed His comfort. I needed His encouragement. I needed to know that He had a plan and that it was good when things were so hard.

I drove to a special pharmacy where I had to pick up additional hormones, expecting to go through the drive-through. I was hoping I would not have to go in—to avoid everyone at all costs. The drive-through was closed. I went in and asked for my prescription. "Oh yes, Mrs. Eastin, let me get the pharmacist." He scanned my hormone shots, the same ones that had cost $5,000 before, and they rang up as $167.00. My husband had new insurance, and the coverage for medications was outstanding. The pharmacist commented. "What excellent insurance you have."

In a small voice, I uttered, "That's what the Lord did for me."

His eyes welled up with tears. I suppose I surprised him by talking about God covering my needs similar to the way others talk about how insurance covers their medicines. He looked me straight in the eye and said, "The miracle has already happened. We just cannot get our mind around it yet."

I was given an unusual opportunity to have a family. I discovered that one of my clients was a surrogate mother. I began to understand that my immune system was working against the in-vitro fertilization pregnancies (IVF) and killing the babies that they put back in my body. Medical science was helpful, but God knew unsearchable things that I did not know. He gave me direction through an exceptionally long and extensive process. Today, I have two healthy and whole biological children carried by different surrogate mothers. I trust that God has the other children that I lost in Heaven with Him.

Miraculously, my first child was born in Houston in the summer of 2008, and my father was present and sober for that birth. One generation ushered in the next. The timing was crucial, because my father was diagnosed with stage-four cancer three months later and passed away twenty-eight days after that. God saw me, transformed me, and touched the situations that meant the most to me.

If I didn't have Christ, I would be hopeless, without direction, and lacking a personal relationship. Now I feel seen, known, and loved. God showed me that I never dropped off His radar. I can trust Him with small personal decisions and with larger important decisions that concern my family and my future.

*Jenni Eastin is a mom of two miracle children, a wife to David, and a believer in the power of a story to connect and encourage others. Jenni engages in meaningful conversations on the Hope Has A Voice podcast. Learn more about her at **JenniEastin.com**.*

Thoughts to Ponder

from Falling Off the Radar

1. God sees you and understands you.

2. You can trust God to help with both small and large decisions.

3. When you call upon God, He will reveal unknowable things.

What things do you need to entrust to God?

"Because he loves me," says the Lord, "I will rescue him; I will protect him, for he acknowledges My name." — Psalm 91:14

A Recycled Life
by Dee Gibbs

Recycling and repurposing are current buzzwords. I have a friend who posts tips about minimizing landfills and waste. She does this every day on Facebook and Instagram. Her posts remind me that we should recycle and repurpose our waste.

There are days when I have felt like trash—used, and worn out—expendable. I have wondered if I could ever be useful again. It wasn't until I began my journey with God that I discovered He was in the business of recycling and repurposing long before modern society saw the need for it.

He is skilled in taking what is broken and making it new. Two scriptures are important to me. One says He knew me before I was born and that He plans for me to do good works. The other says He has a purpose for me, for my well-being, and He wants to give me a hope and a future.

I didn't hear these verses until I was in my early teens, and I was well into my thirties before I truly understood them.

In late October after my eleventh birthday, I was in the sixth grade and had just moved to my fifth school. Once again, I was forced to make new friends. This was the time I was introduced to the Creator and Designer of my purpose.

A new friend invited me to attend church. I went to a group that met every Friday night and Sunday morning. There were over 100 kids from the mid-region of Connecticut. At first, it was more about fun and "fitting in" than learning about God.

On a youth ski trip, one of the counselors assigned to my dorm introduced me to my loving heavenly Father. Alea told me that God loved me and wanted me to spend eternity with Him. All I needed to get right with Him was to admit I had made bad choices called sin. God couldn't be my friend, because I had been His enemy. He expected me to first apologize and accept that His Son was punished for me. Then I could talk to Him and ask for help from Him, Abba Daddy, my biggest fan.

It sounded amazing. I wanted a Father Who would be around, Who I could talk to, Who cared about me, and Who I could go to for advice.

My biological dad worked hard. He had a long train commute on each side of his workday. He was rarely around, and his approval felt like a moving target I could never quite hit.

I shifted from trying to please my earthly father to trying to please my heavenly Father. I studied His Word for a list of dos and don'ts so I could follow the rules and stay in His good graces.

However, I feared His anger and punishment. I still felt dirty, like trash, and unworthy of His love. I felt this way because of the sexual abuse that I had experienced in my early childhood and because of my exposure to pornography. I never told anyone. It was too humiliating. I didn't talk about it with God either. I hoped He would just ignore it, and my guilt would eventually go away. I learned how much God cherished purity, so I was hopeful that if I didn't have sex before marriage, my past would disappear.

My family moved, yet again, in the middle of my high school years. We moved from a simple, country life in New England to the big city of Dallas. I went to college at The University of Oklahoma—again searching for and making new friends. However, I never found a place to call home during my four years there. Because I moved constantly for all those years, I desired to settle down in one place.

I completed a communication degree that would bring a good salary, but the only career path I ever wanted was full-time motherhood. My mom had to work throughout my childhood, and I wanted to be at home raising my kids.

After college, I married a man who attended church in downtown Tulsa. He was a third-generation member of that church. I assumed that meant he was a believer. We didn't discuss his testimony. Because he and his family attended church, this fulfilled the religious checkbox in my premarital list of requirements.

The church messages were mostly history lessons and did not teach how to live a life that was pleasing to God. I attended classes at other area churches . . . constantly seeking. The topics were theological, and we studied denominational differences and current bestselling self-help books.

When my daughter Jennifer was born, my husband took over

his family's engineering business and traveled extensively. While he focused on expanding his sales territory, I was left alone to manage the house and spiritual well-being of our kids.

We grew apart, but I never suspected he would file for divorce and leave. I felt betrayed, hurt, angry, and resentful. I felt lost. My only aspiration was to be a full-time mom, and now I had to find employment. My time with my girls was split with them visiting their Dad.

Later, I was able to look back and see that when Jennifer and Angie were gone, this was quality time for me and the Lord. During those long weekends, I began to see Him as my new husband and provider. He used for good what I dreaded as a disaster.

The divorce left me feeling overwhelmed. I needed my life to be recycled—I needed God. I had prayed for Him to save my marriage many times, but I thought those prayers had fallen on deaf ears. Internally, I was devastated. I was in a crisis of belief.

My married friends and family were clueless about how to advise me. I felt alone. I needed help. *Why didn't God answer my heartfelt sobs and supplications? Was it something I had done? Or hadn't done?* I blamed myself for not being good enough to win my husband back. I was confused and didn't know where to turn. I cried out to God in my despair. *Show me how to get better. I will do anything.* I knew He was a good God, but so many things had happened that weren't good. However, endings are merely new beginnings. New growth was about to burst forth.

A personal invitation to church changed everything. This church emphasized that the Holy Spirit empowers me to live the life God has planned for me. No more rule-following to be loved or trying to be good in my own strength. I had failed miserably at that.

This church taught that prayer was asking God for what we need, but with a new twist. They suggested that I be still and listen for the Lord's guidance. If I prayed, the Holy Spirit would bring God's Word to life, and I would find answers for many of my questions and problems. *What did I have to lose?*

I went back home with a bit of confidence and began job searching again. However, after several days, I felt confused and less certain of myself than ever. I fell from my chair onto the floor and sobbed. My life had taken turns that I was unprepared for, and I had no answers—only more despair. I admitted I needed the Holy Spirit and vowed that if He spoke to me, I would listen and try to obey. The wrestling match was temporarily over. Amazingly, I began to hear what I thought were answers.

I made the deliberate decision to turn my whole life over to God's plans, but I was afraid He might call me out of my comfort zone. So much might change. But the unrest inside of me became greater than my fear, and I chose to trust that God would show me His love. Maybe, just maybe, I could trust Him to lead me beside still waters and refresh my soul. He reassured me of this in Psalm 23.

A Bible study confirmed that God wanted an intimate relationship with me. He was concerned about every detail of my life. *Experiencing God* was a study that taught me to take one day at a time and not worry about tomorrow. It was hard, and I was still terrified of the unknown future, but I focused on the next step. This time, my tears were tears of relief. I could do that.

I tried to pick a career, or course of study for my life, that would allow me to volunteer at my daughters' school, participate in their after-school activities, and spend my entire weekend with them when they came home.

God was going to have to reveal it to me. I couldn't find one thing. *Okay, God, I'm waiting.* I thought of my dancing partners over the years. I realized that a good leader is easy to follow. Maybe with God in the lead, I could relax and let the music of life move me around the dance floor each day. To do this, I had to relinquish my plans—my dance moves—and just step in time with the all-knowing, sovereign God.

He led me to massage therapy and gave me a flexible boss. I only worked when the girls were with their dad. Miracles happen.

I listened and followed through when I felt God was initiating. I saw that God was pursuing me. I just needed to submissively respond. After being rejected like trash, feeling chosen and loved was exhilarating.

God started repurposing my life. The first thing I discerned was that God wanted me to teach His Word. Not being raised in the church as a young child, I was embarrassed when my pastor referred to well-known Old Testament Bible stories that I knew little about. One story was about Jonah being swallowed by a great fish.

That was when a lead-teacher position opened up in the two-year-old's class, and the church contacted me. *Just my speed,* was my thought as I rolled my eyes and laughed out loud. I learned the basics of the Old Testament characters by reading board books to the toddlers. They were never as interested in the storyline as I was.

My curiosity led me to study the Old Testament for many years. Because I was excited about what I was uncovering, I shared the lessons and principles enthusiastically with anyone willing to listen. I was invited to teach in many adult Sunday school classes.

I suspect it was old news to them, but it was exciting and fresh to me. God performed a miracle in me to touch lives. Who would have guessed this unchurched girl would be a Bible teacher?

During the same time, I sensed that God was repurposing me to counsel others. I pursued all the available avenues. I was given a scholarship to attend a local seminary, but after a year, that path did not seem right. I watched and waited for other opportunities.

At my massage therapy job, I realized I was already counseling people who were going through hard times. It was a start. As my clients talked with me about their problems, God brought to my memory many of the Old Testament characters who had similar problems. We would discuss how that story related to their lives.

However, I still sensed I needed to get a degree or more training. I followed several rabbit trails, but nothing worked. Ten years later, I wandered into a church classroom on a Sunday morning and heard a guest speaker talk about a school that offered training for pastoral counseling. I pursued more information and found that everything fit my schedule. Three years later, I finished my training and was officially counseling. Sometimes, just like Abraham, God hints to us what will happen in the future, but it is years before it comes to pass.

My third repurposing was to write a book. I had written poetry as a ten- to thirteen-year-old child and sent many poems to *Reader's Digest* and other magazines. None were published. In 2011, I felt prompted to go to my family cabin in the arid desert of southern Colorado and start writing a book. Three summers in a row, I spent a month there. God gave me insights as I researched and studied His Word. The scripture that impressed me was Hosea 2:14: "I am now going to allure her; I will lead her into the wilderness and speak tenderly to her." Each time I returned home, I added more folders to my book box. I still have that box in my office, where it has been sitting untouched for the last five years. Life happens.

My faith in God has grown since then. I have learned that when He says something, He follows through in His timing, not mine. Also, I need to be willing to step out of my comfort zone. Each season of growth brings uncertainty, and I must listen to what God says, and believe that I can move to the next level.

Many times, tapes of conversations in my past run through my head. Feelings of unworthiness creep in to paralyze me. God is always patient in my doubt and brings encouragers to me. When I do not have self-assurance, others' kind words give me the confidence to do what God wants. I also ask the Holy Spirit to prompt me to speak blessings and encouragement over others.

Are you anything like me? Have you ever been broken by life circumstances? Have you felt like trash, like a total failure with no hope? He meets us where we are when we call to Him. In the Bible, God says that when you seek Him, you will find Him, provided you seek Him wholeheartedly.

Have you relinquished your dreams for His plans? My dreams seemed ripped from my hands, but in the end, I was a much better mom because I had the time to focus on knowing God better. His dreams have taken me places I never would have gone. Surrendering to do His will has brought me to a place of deeper peace and communion with Him.

Whatever you are going through, know that God has a next "step," maybe even a "leap" of faith for you. Let Him lead when the two of you dance. He is repurposing and recycling your hurts and broken pieces into a new you.

Dee Gibbs has followed God's lead to teach adult Bible studies, weekly classes, and retreats and conferences for over twenty-five years. Her mission is to unite the family of God (by breaking down denominational barriers between Jews and Christians) and mature them with biblical training. Her current project is writing a Bible study manual for Christian believers on the biblical Sabbaths and the Feasts of the Lord. Follow her blogs on Facebook, Denise Dee Lytle Gibbs.

Thoughts to Ponder
from A Recycled Life

1. God skillfully takes brokenness to make something new.

2. Repurposing lives is God's specialty.

3. Surrendering to God and His will brings deep peace.

What areas of your life need recycling or repurposing?

See, I am doing a new thing! Now it springs up;
do you not perceive it? I am making a way in the wilderness
and streams in the wasteland. — Isaiah 43:19

My True Name
by Sarah Pittmann

Have you ever felt *less* than what you wanted to feel? Broken, worthless, unwanted, less-than, scum, unloved? That is how I felt in my late twenties. I had not intended or expected life to go this direction. I tried to make all the right choices along the way—tried to be better than the past I came from. For a time, I was the eternal optimist, happy, always smiling. But who was this person looking back at me in the mirror? This reflection looked jaded, bitter, hopeless, quick to lash out with anger, depressed, full of darkness, pain, and hurt inflicted by others . . . who made me think I was the problem.

I couldn't tell what was right and wrong anymore. Too many messages received by a few individuals, either verbal or nonverbal, overwrote my identity. I was not whole, healthy, and strong. I made poor choices. I was hurt and wronged along the way, but I let a few voices have power over my identity and life. I did not know better. I had lost my way and no longer had an anchor. I didn't know what voices to let in and what voices to reject.

I came from a broken past. My father was controlling and was abusive to my mom. He skewed our view of things, claiming to be the only true Christian, yet acting opposite to what the Bible taught. He took verses out of context to authorize his actions. But God interjected a good foundation. Living in a remote location, my Mom homeschooled us three girls, including teaching us to read the whole Bible, not just part of it. I praise the Lord that she taught us in our early years. The Word of God was written onto our hearts, telling us we were loved and in need of salvation. We asked God into our hearts as little girls. The foundation of my life was poured.

However, my identity was not secure. I did not understand the true love of God the Father, because my earthly father did not show love. He tried to play God by changing my name in an attempt to change my identity. He did not love or accept me for who I was. He tried to control and change me into *his* vision of a perfect child. Maybe it was because they had expected a boy, and he got me instead. Maybe it was simply the way I was uniquely me. Whatever the reason, he delivered the message that I was wrong for being who I was.

I was an exuberant girl, who wore her emotions on her sleeve and delighted in the joy of life and discovery. But that didn't fit the mold of a passive, quiet, and submissive little girl that he had in mind. So he tried to crush my character, to beat back the parts of me that made me who I was. Despite his constant teardowns, I was unable to put on a mask and hide who I really was. I was honest to a fault. I was all me, upfront, all the time. When I was almost five years old, my dad learned that my middle name, Nicole, meant "victory of the people," and he decided that changing my name would change who I was and solve the problem of controlling me. What better name than Abigail, which means "father's joy," to give the power to him to gain victory over my character and identity.

My mom was so sweet though. She made it a fun thing and presented it to me as meaning "Daddy's girl," since I was the tomboy and was always helping Dad with chores (even though it was not always my choice). My new name was a "gift" to me on my fifth birthday. However, when man tries to play God, it only ends in destruction. Later in life, for fear of being beaten down for who I really was, I unintentionally allowed others to rewrite my identity as a matter of survival.

My mom divorced my dad when I was nine years old. We were no longer secluded and living in the middle of nowhere. We started public school, went to church, and lived in neighborhoods. For a time, I was a good church girl. My faith and confidence started to grow, and I was happy. However, I was naïve, and lots of messages of who I should be flew at me from all directions. The house of me had a frame but no walls. So everything that tried to blow in, got in. I tried to block out things I knew were wrong, but sooner or later, with no walls, it all got in. I found myself taking up residence, or "making friends," with the ways of the world and compromising my morals. But God protected me from many things amid my poor decisions through high school. When I got married a year later, I changed my middle name back to Nicole so my name was no longer connected to my birth father.

Married young and in college, the pull of God, along with the pull of the world, was too much. Something had to give. As the Bible says, you cannot serve two masters. Sadly, I chose the world. I was seduced by the small measure of power I found in igniting lust in others. But I was deceived. I wasn't gaining power. I was walking into bondage, and I was losing my identity.

Furthermore, without being continually well-rooted in God's Word and God's truth, all religions and spiritualisms sounded alike. Looking back, I can tell you with certainty, that it was a lie of the enemy. In my darkness, I couldn't see it. I kept sinking into the miry pit, little by little, not realizing I was sliding until it was too late. I couldn't find a way out.

My husband, a Christian by faith but hurt by the church, had run as far as he could in living the ways of the world. He dragged me farther into darkness. My fractured self willingly followed. Our marriage was rough, and many times we came close to not making it. Being married so young, neither of us knew who we were or how to do things right. Both of us were broken from childhood.

Over the years, my husband poked at me with his opinionated definitions of who I was. Though he would say he was joking, his words rang true in my ears. His video games held precedence over me. And three words, "I don't care," were his jaded response to almost anything I tried to talk to him about. The messages I received told me I was worthless, unwanted, and unloved. And when you don't know who you are, if you hear something long enough, you start to believe you are those things. They became my identity.

There were a few years we both had decent jobs, lived well, and had a good marriage with few fights. Yet depression kept trying to overwhelm me. You see, God was not part of our equation. It didn't matter if times were good or times were bad. I had a gaping hole inside of me that nothing in this world could fill. I prayed occasionally and felt an echo of what I once knew in God—wholeness.

But my pride and fear would not let me return. Pride, because I would have to humble myself and acknowledge my wrong choices, as I walked the wrong path. Fear, because of what others around me would think: I was not a good Christian girl anymore. I didn't keep company with anyone who was, and I didn't want to be mocked.

But God called me back to Himself. The bottom dropped out from underneath us financially. Our marriage deteriorated. We had a one-and-a-half-year-old, sweet little boy, and I was pregnant with our little girl. I was in the deepest, darkest pit imaginable—full of despair, depression, anxiety, and hopelessness. The psalmist calls it a miry pit. But it was this very pit that led me to church again after so many years. I wanted my little boy to know how to be saved and go to Heaven. At that point, I didn't have a clue how to tell him about God. Out of desperation and fear, along with wanting to find some playmates for him, I went to Blue Oaks Baptist Church in Rocklin, California.

I went by myself. My husband was on the road, trucking, and he wouldn't have come anyway. I struggled to smile as I greeted new people and dropped my little boy off in the kid's area. Seated by myself in one of the back rows, I felt empty, like a dried-out husk—fragile, brittle, and ready to crumble. I didn't know if I would find an old hypocritical message of why their form of Christianity was the best, or if there was going to be something real to find.

We sang some songs, and then the pastor preached. God plucked at my heartstrings, speaking to my inner being. Tears streamed down my face as the pastor's words spoke directly to me. I knew the only safe place for my shattered self was in God's hands. I kept returning to church. It was like a droplet of cool, living water to my parched soul. I found hope and a reason to keep on living. I grew strong again.

Then we moved to Texas. We left most of our belongings behind, because we could only afford a small trailer. I didn't want to lose what I had recently found, so my top priority was finding another church with authentic Christians who were preaching and living the truth of God's Word.

After a quick Google search, I tried a nearby church that sounded good according to their website. I was eight-and-a-half months pregnant, with a toddler at my side. I walked into Hulen Street Church in Fort Worth, Texas, while my husband was either working or sleeping. I'm not sure which. But when the sermon was identical to the one I heard in California, I knew it was the right church. I didn't need to shop around. Having no family or friends in the area, I needed to get to know people fast. I was about to have a baby.

I joined the women's Bible study a few days later. By midweek, I had a support group. Those ladies loved me and my family well. They took care of us and donated most of what we had lost in our move. They acted out the hands and feet of Jesus. I'm so grateful for those ladies at Hulen Street, who showed me how to live my faith 24/7, not just on weekends.

Bible study dispelled my misconceptions about God and the Bible, as well as my small ideas of what it meant to be a Christian. If you're not active in a group Bible study, I strongly suggest you find one. Church was water to my soul and strength to my bones. I fell in love with Jesus. My heart filled with joy. Peace reigned in my mind and emotions. I learned I was free to not sin. God also taught me what a father's love is. I became a daughter for the first time in my life. My true identity is daughter of the Most High King.

My husband came to church for a little while, but the intimacy scared him. He threw all his walls back up and added a few more. He pushed hard against God. He shut out the church again—and shut me out too. The closer I drew to God and the more peace I seemed to have, the angrier he became. Spiritual warfare ran rampant in our house. The verbal and emotional hurt from my husband that had ebbed and flowed throughout our marriage grew intense and manifested physically on one occasion.

But God strengthened me and matured me through all this. Instead of seeking my worth in my husband, I now found my worth and identity in Christ Jesus, my first love and true Bridegroom. I vividly remember when God revealed to me that the hardship was more than a rough marriage. It was abuse. God loves me so much, this was not what He wanted for His daughters. I refused the thought of divorce, because I didn't want a broken family like I had when I was growing up.

God showed me that the stain of abuse is worse than the stain of divorce. I knew our marriage was on the line, that I had to stand against the abuse and say, "No more." To do so was terrifying. With much prayer, counsel with a church elder, and support of a godly mentor and friend, we came up with a plan.

The moment I stood and spoke, the Holy Spirit calmed me and helped me speak. I was given an extra measure of faith that fateful night in October 2017. I perceived in my spirit that the great I Am was standing behind me, fighting the spiritual battle. Then the darkness disappeared from my husband's eyes. God fought for me, fought for my husband, and fought for us.

We still have our ups and downs, along with viciously hard struggles in the healing process. We have a long way to go, but I'm happy to report that there has not been any more abuse, and we are still married. The Lord is good. Had it not been as bad as it was, I would not have seen the miracles God has done in my husband. He decided to try Bible study for a few weeks, and now he meets somewhat regularly with a mentor from the church he once chastised greatly. "Come and see what the Lord has done, the desolations He has brought on the earth. He makes wars cease to the ends of the earth. He breaks the bow and shatters the spear; He burns the shields with fire. He says, 'Be still, and know that I am God'" (Psalm 46:8-10).

Deuteronomy 26:8 says, "The Lord brought us out of Egypt with a mighty hand." Egypt represents Israel's slavery or bondage. If we personalize, it reads something like this: "The Lord delivered us out of bondage with a mighty hand." The bondage the Lord delivered me from included fear, lack of self-worth, an abusive marriage, chains from childhood, selfishness, lustful desires, anxiety, anger, depression, covetousness, worry, and lesser gods (like the opinions of other people).

My earthly father may have tried to shape and mold me, but God, my heavenly Father, designed me and told me who I truly am. Now I praise God on High. His praise will ever be on my lips, for in Him is my identity, and in Him my worth is found. In God alone, I am secure and have all I need.

A fire burns inside me these days, full of passion for the Lord and for the hurting and broken people who need Him, the same way I need Him. I am lit up with His light and truth. My old self wouldn't recognize the "me" of today. I have both hands raised in church, and I have a date with the King of all creation every morning. God healed my broken heart and brought me into my true identity. God created me as uniquely me, and I belong to Him. I'm a vibrant mess. Some might think I'm a little over the top in love with Jesus. But if you knew the depths of the darkness that He saved me from, you would understand the tenacity of my worship and the fervency with which I tell others.

I found the real deal. I have seen too much of God's work in the little puzzle pieces of my life, as well as the big miracles in my marriage, to deny that He alone is God, the answer to everything.

Here is my identity now. I am healed. I am whole. I am loved. I belong. I am wanted. I am cherished. I am desired. I am full of joy. I have peace. I have purpose. I am strong. I am secure. I am protected. I am comforted. I am known. I am a daughter and a wife to the King on high. I invite you to make these characteristics your identity too, through faith in Jesus Christ. God restored my identity. He can restore yours. "With God all things are possible" (Matthew 19:26).

*Sarah Pittmann is a daughter of God, a mom of two precious children, ages seven and nine, and a wife to her husband for eighteen years. A former math teacher, she now lives in Fort Worth, Texas, and currently works as a Client Invoice Specialist for Huckabee Architects, Inc. She invoices school districts across Texas for the design of learning environments focused on the success of all students. She is active in her church, intentionally takes every opportunity to disciple her kids along the path of life, and has a passion to encourage women to thrive in their faith. Contact Sarah at **Sarah@ShoulderWarriors.com** or view her website and blog at **ShoulderWarriors.com.***

Thoughts to Ponder
from My True Name

1. God is the source of your identity.

2. The world will leave you wanting and broken, but God will satisfy, heal, and make you whole.

3. In Christ, you are loved, you belong, you are greatly desired, and you are secure.

What is God teaching you about your identity?

My soul rejoices in my God. For he has clothed me with garments of salvation and arrayed me in a robe of his righteousness. — Isaiah 61:10

The Hole in My Heart
by Heather Dennis

In Minnesota where I grew up, we had a saying: "There are two seasons—winter and construction." The snow and ice from the winter months left the roads riddled with potholes, and the short summers didn't offer much time for road crews to fix them. Try and try as they might to fill them, winter returned and more potholes appeared. My life experiences, just like those Minnesota roads, left holes in my heart. And try and try as I might to fill them myself, they only grew bigger and deeper.

My parents divorced when I was five. I didn't understand why my mom and dad didn't live together anymore. I only saw my dad twice a week, Sundays and Wednesdays for church. I was a girl in need of her father's love and affection. The divorce was hard on me and left a hole in my heart, which was filled with sadness.

When I was twelve, my dad moved to Texas and my mom remarried. Because of the difficulties, I started fighting with my mom. The only place I felt comfort was at church. I had a wonderful group of friends and accepted the Christian faith as my own. Even though the hole in my heart had grown bigger, going to church and being surrounded by my friends helped.

Because fighting with my mom and stepdad was unbearable, I moved to Texas to live with my dad when I was sixteen. I thought that would solve all my problems. However, running away from my problems didn't solve them. You see, I still had the hole in my heart.

Unfortunately, I didn't fit in at the church my dad and stepmom attended. I was hurt. I thought, *If this is what church is like in Texas, then I just won't go.* I was certain the reason I was hurting was that I had no control over my life. I longed for the day when I would turn eighteen, graduate from high school, and move out on my own.

When I went to college, I thought, *Finally! Freedom! I can run my life my way. That'll solve all my problems.* I did not honor God with my lifestyle in college. During the last two years of college, I lived with the man who later became my first husband. By marrying him, I thought I could right the wrongs I had done. However, there were no right things I could ever do that would undo the wrong things I had done.

Our marriage wasn't founded on God, and I don't believe my husband was a believer. I became an agnostic. We let sin rule our lives. My husband had a wandering eye that caused tremendous pain in our marriage. I felt insecure, unloved, and unattractive. The disgust I felt for him grew so strong that I divorced him within five years.

I left that marriage with mixed emotions. On the one hand, I harbored anger, sadness, and resentment. On the other hand, I felt newfound freedom, having broken away from the bondage of that marriage. I did not honor God with my newfound freedom.

I soon met Jason, the man who became my second husband. I fell in love with him hard and fast. He was charming and funny—the kind of guy who never met a stranger. He was loveable and a servant leader. Everybody loved him.

Just three months after we met, Jason was diagnosed with young-onset Parkinson's disease. He was only thirty-three. He said, "Listen, I've got this for life. You have your whole life ahead. You don't need to stick around. You're not obligated to me." That was the kind of guy he was. But I was so in love with him, I didn't leave.

We married, and the first couple of years of his disease weren't bad. He saw the right specialist, who prescribed the right medications. For a while, things were good, but then his Parkinson's got worse. Because it is a progressive disease, the doctors kept prescribing higher doses and additional medications. This affected his sleep. When his medications wore off, he awakened in the middle of the night with stiff muscles.

At that time, my radio station had a contest in honor of Martin Luther King, Jr. called "I Have a Dream." People wrote to the station and shared their dream. Then they picked a few dreams to grant.

So I wrote in and said my dream was for my husband to dream again. I explained in my letter that he was an eight-year veteran of the United States Marine Corps and was diagnosed with young-onset Parkinson's disease. The disease was affecting his sleep. I thought the small gesture of getting a new mattress might help him sleep a little better at night.

The contest came and went, and I didn't hear from the radio station. I shrugged it off thinking, *Oh well, nothing ventured, nothing gained.* A month went by. Then out of the blue, the radio station called me. They said they read my letter and wanted to grant my wish. Jason and I went to the radio station and got to share our story and about our fundraiser on the air. Then they gave us a new mattress.

Two months later, a fundraiser was held for the Michael J. Fox Foundation Parkinson's Research. The guest speaker was David Vobora. David founded a nonprofit called the Adaptive Training Foundation (ATF), which helped veterans with limb amputations go through physical training to improve their strength, mobility, and independence. Jason saw that David was wearing a black ring on his pointer finger, the same kind that Jason wore. The ring was from another nonprofit called 22Kill. The organization raises awareness for veteran Post Traumatic Stress Disorder (PTSD) and veteran suicide. Jason said, "I'm going to go introduce myself to David."

David was a former NFL linebacker, and he looked ten feet tall and bullet-proof. I was intimidated and told Jason, "You go right ahead."

Jason walked up to David and showed him his ring. They fist-bumped and had what I can only call a "bro moment."

David encouraged Jason to apply for the upcoming class at ATF, which led to Jason's acceptance into the program. By that time, Jason had difficulty tying his shoes, getting dressed, and brushing his teeth. Even things like eating a bowl of cereal were hard. As a former Marine, he felt like he could take on the entire world. Even though he was one of the most positive people I knew, Parkinson's took a toll. What ATF did for Jason was more than just improve his physical ability. It gave him a renewed outlook on life.

I thought, *I have my husband back.*

Jason graduated from ATF in August 2016.

My grandmother, who was in the final stages of her life, passed away. This was the first person I lost who had a profound impact on me. I grew close to her in my twenties and early thirties. She was a devout Christian and believed she was going to Heaven. I wanted desperately to believe that too.

Sunday after the funeral, Jason flew home, and I flew out on a business trip. That night Jason planned to go to church with David Vobora. Because he was speaking, David invited everyone from ATF to go to his church. Jason told me the service was wonderful and we should go to that church. Then we talked about going to church, starting a family, and raising our kids in church. I said, "Okay, sure, we can go to that church."

Two days later, on Tuesday, September 13, 2016, I got a phone call from Jason's cousin. I was at Chicago O'Hare airport about to board my flight. He said Jason had driven his car off the road and paramedics were taking him to the hospital.

The way he described the accident, it sounded minor. I assumed it was protocol for paramedics to take him to the hospital to get checked out before going home. I talked to one of the paramedics and told him about Jason's condition and medications. Then I called my parents and Jason's parents and asked them to go to the hospital to check on Jason.

When I landed in St. Louis, I went to the baggage claim and called my dad.

Dad said, "Jason's very sick. You need to come home now."

Sick? Sick? What do you mean he's sick? I didn't understand. *He got a little shaken up from running his car off the road into a field. How could he be sick?*

I spoke to the ER doctor while I was still at the airport. She said his temperature was 106 when he arrived at the hospital.

I told her I didn't understand, and I didn't think people survived temperatures that high. She said they got his temperature down, but there were still a lot of unanswered questions.

I prayed to God that night for the first time in over a decade. I begged God to save my husband—to heal him. It was going to be hard recovering from this, but we'd do whatever it took to figure it out.

The next day, I went straight to the hospital. David Vobora, who had been there all night, met me and took me to Jason. I wasn't prepared for what I saw. My husband was unconscious and hooked to IVs, tubes, and monitors.

The doctors said he had a lot of toxins in his system. As a result of the high temperature, his muscles were breaking down. His kidneys and liver were trying to clear the toxins, but they were also talking about putting him on dialysis. Then his heart stopped. The doctors and nurses rushed in to revive him and were successful. However, one by one his organs started to fail. I held his hand all night and begged and pleaded with God, *Please, save my husband.*

The doctors didn't think Jason would make it to the next morning, and when he did, I thought we had reached a turning point. However, they told me they'd done all they could. All his organs had failed. The last to go would be his heart, and it was about to fail. So I climbed into the hospital bed with him and held him. I listened to his breathing until he took his last breath.

I lay there and cried and cried. And just like that, I became a thirty-one-year-old widow. I needed help. I needed God.

After the funeral, I went to church and began seeing a counselor. That hole in my heart was so big and so wide. I desperately wanted to numb the pain, so I tried to do it in ways that did not honor God. Through all of that, I learned in my grief that God was always with me. Even when I didn't see Him, He never left me.

Nothing happens by chance. God always has a plan and a purpose. I learned that a woman named Sarah, David Vobora's wife, had listened to the radio program when Jason and I were interviewed for the "I Have a Dream" contest. Our story resonated with her because her grandfather also had Parkinson's. She said to David, "We should change the mission statement of our nonprofit, so we can help guys like Jason." And they did.

In hindsight, I realized that Jason and I "happened" to meet David Vobora. This led to Jason going through ATF and David inviting Jason to church. The night Jason went to church, he accepted Christ as his personal Lord and Savior—just two days before the accident. What a gift it was to know, without a doubt, that Jason was in Heaven. You see, God never leaves us.

For seven months, my grief consumed me even though I was going to church every Sunday. I felt God tugging at my heartstrings, saying, *Just give your life to me. Trust me.* But I was torn between the world where I felt I had control and a world where I needed to give control to God and trust Him.

I went to the Good Friday service at my church, and the pastor described what Jesus did for me. Jesus, the Son of God, came to Earth as a baby. He lived the perfect life and was a spotless lamb. He suffered and died on the cross for me. His blood was shed on Calvary for me. I saw, for the first time, what Jesus did for me. At that moment, I fully trusted in God. He loved me so much He sent His Son to save me. I was redeemed.

Two days later, on Easter, the pastor said he planned to baptize new believers. I was the first to sign up. My heart had already changed. My heart was washed clean, but I wanted to show the world that I was a new person.

God restored me. In the middle of my grief, I never thought I would be healed or remarry. But God did heal me and brought a man to me whose heart searched after God. A man who knew the true love of God and loved me. I believed that you can't love other people until you know the true *agape* love of God. Not only did God bring this man into my life, but He also blessed us with our very own baby girl.

God is good. God healed that big hole in my heart, which I had tried in vain to fill for so many years. There is nothing under the sun you can do to fill the hole in your heart. I tried it all. But God will heal your heart if you let Him. He will heal all the hurts and pains in your life.

All you have to do is say, "God, I'm hurting. I'm in so much pain right now, and I've tried everything to make the pain go away. But I realize I need You. I'm so sorry for all the things I've done. Thank You for sending Your Son Jesus to take away my sins. God, I trust in You, and I'm giving myself to You. From this day forward, I put my faith in You."

God is faithful to His Word. If you prayed that prayer in your heart, He will heal the hole in your heart and restore you.

Heather Dennis *was born in Minnesota and lived there for sixteen years until she moved to Texas, where she's lived ever since. She went to the University of Texas at Dallas and studied Neuroscience and Geology. She works as a Sales Director for a large healthcare company. She is married to* *her husband, Beck. They have a beautiful baby girl named Sarah. In her free time, Heather enjoys traveling and hiking, especially in our National Parks.*

Thoughts to Ponder
from The Hole in My Heart

1. God purpose is better than you can plan.

2. Jesus heals the deepest wounds.

3. God is a heart-surgery specialist.

What hole in your heart does God need to heal?

He heals the brokenhearted and binds up their wounds. — Psalm 147:3

Buffering

by Cheri McKean

Get up. No, it's not time for work but time to give the appearance that today has a purpose and a plan. Let's see . . . I take a shower and check off this first task. Next, I feed the dog and take her out, drink my cup of tea, and then sit at the computer so it feels like I am working. How many more tasks can I invent until I feel productive and useful today?

The coronavirus pandemic caused governments around the globe to issue stay-at-home orders. Some might equate "safer at home" to the classic film, *Groundhog Day*. Not me. I feel like my life is stalled—spinning like the buffering dial on the screen, when the movie stops and the viewer sits and waits, hoping the data loads faster so that the rest of the story is revealed.

As with the rest of the world, my life has recently buffered along. I know I'm not the only one who has had her world paused, but I sure feel like it. My thirty-two-year career has been with a major retail department store. Working from home was weird, but surprisingly doable. Shortly into the new normal, on a Tuesday conference call titled "Business Update," I was informed that I was being furloughed. That means "leave of absence, without pay." I was devastated that it had come to this—it was inconceivable.

A few days later, I received notification that I was eligible for voluntary early retirement—a blessing and a curse. A blessing that in these uncertain economic times I could choose to retire rather than risk being laid off. A curse at my age, because I would still need to find employment to supplement the monthly retirement pay that was significantly less than my current salary.

The news created in me a host of emotions, including worry, pride, and insecurity. In my attempt to make sense of this upheaval, I struggled with my human shortcomings, trying to reconcile them with what I knew to be true of God's promises. As I examined my feelings, I found comfort in God's Word. Even though I reverted to my fears again and again, I found the security of His presence and assurance of comfort, peace, and provision in His Holy Word. It was the lamp shining into the shadows of my uncertainty, reassuring me of His presence in all my weaknesses. "The Word of God is alive and active. Sharper than any double-edged sword, it penetrates even to dividing soul and spirit, joints and marrow; it judges the thoughts and attitudes of the heart" (Hebrews 4:12).

Worry: that sneaky transgression that consumes and blinds our ability to trust our heavenly Father and the path He has yet to reveal. Worry was my biggest struggle, especially about finances. After thirty-two years, I had achieved a comfortable salary and generous vacation time that allowed my husband and me to travel with friends and live a contented life. It provided the ability to be generous when the opportunity arose. It also gave me a feeling of being worthy in the eyes of my husband, my kids, our family, and friends. In hindsight, I see that it became a huge piece of my identity.

Worry overtook the logic and belief that I knew to be true and set me on a road to self-reliance. Suddenly, I got into a "fixer" mode. I needed to find a job, but:

- How would I find a job that could replace my current income?
- Could I get the same amount of vacation time?
- Did I want to do the same type of work?
- Maybe I should do something different, but what could I do?
- Was I good enough to be considered by a new employer?
- How long would it be until I found a job?
- What would I do about insurance?
- How long would we need to adjust our lifestyle?
- What would our friends think when we turned down a trip or a nice dinner out?
- What would my kids think of us?

The worries began to consume every thought and cloud my connection to the One Who is sovereign and could carry this burden and relieve my anxiety. I knew His promises. I had claimed them repeatedly, and yet in my human weakness, I still doubted that He could make this right—at least my version of "right." That was the flaw, and I knew it, but I was still intent on accomplishing my version of where my path should lead instead of surrendering my heart, mind, and life to the vision and path of what He had planned for me. "Humble yourselves, therefore, under God's mighty hand, that He may lift you up in due time. Cast all your anxiety on Him because He cares for you (1 Peter 5:6–7).

Pride: not only arrogance but preferring self-will to God's will. I had always been proud of my accomplishments and the work I had done. After starting my career, I achieved more than I could have ever dreamed of. The path was not always easy. I made a lot of sacrifices. So did my family. There were some difficult and low times, but that was balanced by the love I had for my job and the people I encountered and worked with through the years. I was recognized and rewarded in many areas of my work. When work was tough, my God carried me through those times. I was always able to reflect and see where He sustained me through the storms, even though I might not have been aware of His presence at the time.

I once told someone that my job did not define me. I felt confident in that statement then, but now as I maneuver through this new season of life, I am not so sure. My job defined me to some extent—but I was wrong to let it do so. My success had nothing to do with me—it was thirty-two years of God's continuing provision and plan. And yet I conveyed my skills and achievements to others in self-reliant words and descriptors. I especially loved how captivated they seemed as I described my accomplishments, connections, and abilities. "Do nothing out of selfish ambition or vain conceit. Rather, in humility value others above yourselves" (Philippians 2:3).

Insecurity: self-doubt that creates a sinkhole in which one constantly falls into, struggles, and needs rescue from, to escape. I am a middle child, and I believe there is some basis for the theory of middle child syndrome—the feeling of being left out and always trying to be the peacemaker and pleaser. This has been an inner struggle that I have disguised my entire life. While hiding my inner fears and insecurities, I pushed myself to participate in and strive for activities or positions that gave the appearance of confidence and knowledge. I was afraid that someone would discover that I am not that confident person I pretended to be but was not deserving of nor was I that smart. I constantly feared that my inadequacies would be revealed. This feeling has permeated my life.

- Straight A's weren't enough. I wasn't that smart— probably just lucky.
- Graduating third in my high school class—boy, did I have them fooled.
- A full academic scholarship to college—someone must have been looking out for me.
- A major retailer hiring me—it was because of a family friend—it couldn't have been my abilities.
- Raising three kids while balancing a career—by the skin of my teeth with continuous feelings of failure at home and work, trying so hard to give the appearance that I could do it all, while going to bed at night feeling like a loser.

Oh, I could go on and on. It all sounds so self-serving. But I know I wasn't alone. God sustained me. I reached out to Him daily. I prayed that He would help me overcome. I prayed for peace and wisdom. He did not disappoint. I know this is how He made me. He knew I needed to rely on His strength to carry me through. He blessed me. His Word and promises sustained me. He surrounded me with praying family and friends, and He never left me. I have never been "cured" of this insecurity. It has and always will be a struggle that only God can heal every hour of every day. "Be strong and courageous. Do not be afraid; do not be discouraged, for the Lord, your God will be with you wherever you go" (Joshua 1:9).

All these thoughts fill my mind. Sometimes they are so loud it seems that I can't feel God's presence or hear His guidance. At times, the screen of my life is overshadowed by the stalled buffering rotation, halting the expected revelation of the next scene.

- What is God's plan for me?
- What is the purpose of this next season of my life?
- I wish I had a clue, a sign, or something to show me what tomorrow holds.

- What will my life look like tomorrow?
- What job is waiting for me?
- How will we adjust to this altered lifestyle?

During this time of reflection, it is abundantly clear that I cannot continue in this vein without utter dependence on my heavenly Father. I will not have peace, security, or direction without surrendering to Him. I must wake up every morning and renew my faith, my trust, and my entire self to Him. He is my salvation today. He is the God of my past, and He holds my future. But He equips me for today. It is not His intent for me to borrow trouble from tomorrow. When tomorrow comes, He will be there with me, revealing His plans and intentions for the day. I can claim His peace today. Tomorrow, He will unveil the new day and the new plan, buffering just enough to show the part allotted for that day. "Show me Your ways, Lord, teach me Your paths. Guide me in Your truth and teach me, for You are God my Savior, and my hope is in You all day long" (Psalm 25:4-5).

Why do I approach this new season with fear? I know my God is able, and yet I always feel like He needs my help . . . my suggestions . . . my manipulation. Who am I to assume that God needs any help at all? I am not more powerful than God. No, the issue is me. It is my need for control and my inability to surrender to His will—to trust Him completely in every part of my life, big and small. I pray that God will show me what job I should pursue, and yet I sit at the computer and begin to form my plan and strategy. I try to decide the salary range that works for my current lifestyle. I ignore job descriptions that might pose a challenge. I look for easy and comfortable. Surely God would not want me to put myself out there, reaching for something unfamiliar that would threaten my "safe" life.

I must learn to wait on Him. I know this, and I fall into the same trap of self-reliance. I am shackled by the chains of my own choosing. I know what I should be doing and in Whom I should place my trust, but I seem to find security in this prison because I control it. Why do I do this? I remember times when I broke free from my self-imposed restraints, and then I eventually slipped back into them. It is only through God's grace and divine intervention that I know His will prevails. I will have that moment of clarity. I will stop and cling to His offering. I pray that my surrender will cover me with the blanket of peace and assurance that comes only from His hand. "Some sat in darkness, in utter darkness, prisoners suffering in iron chains, because they rebelled against God's commands and despised the plans of the Most High. So He subjected them to bitter labor; they stumbled, and there was no one to help. Then they cried to the Lord in their trouble, and He saved them from their distress. He brought them out of darkness, the utter darkness, and broke away their chains" (Psalm 107:10–14).

I may be anxious tomorrow, worried about what comes next, but I will turn to Him for peace. I may be embarrassed to admit that I am unemployed, but I will claim God's provision. I may be insecure about my skills for the next job, but I will seek His wisdom and pray for the power of confidence that can be found only in the security of His love for me. When my life seems buffered, put on hold, waiting for the next scene to be revealed, I will trust in Him. "For I know the plans I have for you," declares the Lord, "plans to prosper you and not to harm you, plans to give you hope and a future. Then you will call on Me and come and pray to Me, and I will listen to you. You will seek Me and find Me when you seek Me with all your heart" (Jeremiah 29:11–13).

Cheri McKean *is wife and mother of three, mother-in-law of one, and grandmother of two. She lives in Frisco, Texas, and has been a long-time active member of Frisco First Baptist Church. She loves to travel with her husband and friends. Her plan to be an English teacher was never realized but was replaced by a successful and adventurous career with a national retailer. Retirement has opened the door for her to pursue a lifelong dream of becoming an author.*

Thoughts to Ponder
from Buffering

1. Worry hinders your trust in your heavenly Father.

2. Pride causes you to rely on yourself rather than God.

3. Your identity is based on who God says you are.

What anxious thoughts should you turn over to God?

Do not worry about tomorrow, for tomorrow will worry about itself. Each day has enough trouble of its own. — Matthew 6:34

Mental Illness
and a Near-Miss Bullet
by Debra Moore

There was no outward appearance of mental health difficulty in her appearance. Anyone observing my mother at the time, would have said she was a typical young lady who had grown up to be beautiful and kind. My mother, Charlene Lavanna Polk, was a tall, quiet southern belle beauty with pretty blonde hair and pale blue eyes. She loved God and was a member of the neighborhood Church of Christ.

After she graduated from Murphy High School, she was hired as a secretary at Brookley Field Air Force Base in Mobile, Alabama and met my father, Allen Zesewitz, stationed in the Air Force there. He was a northerner from Philadelphia, and they started dating and became close. He represented something and someone different from her troubled Southern family.

When she was a young girl, she sat at her father's feet and watched Alabama Crimson Tide football games. This infuriated her mother, my maternal grandmother, Faye Polk, who was deathly jealous of any relationship my mother had with her father, Edgar Polk Sr. My grandmother could not stand her three daughters. However, she lavished praise and love on her three sons. This unequal treatment created dysfunction in their family. My mother and her siblings were beaten by her mother. In the 1950's this might have been acceptable, although morally wrong. My mother told me that her grandmother, who they called, Big Mama even though she was only five feet tall, loved her very much. They lived in rural Mississippi, and when she and her siblings visited their grandparent's home, wild horses came to the porch for apples and sugar cubes. Big Mama provided my mother with love and compassion, and she could never understand why her daughter, Faye Polk, was mean and hateful to her daughters.

In the early years of my childhood, Mom pre-schooled me at home. She had bins of manipulatives such as blocks, books, and crayons, which she used to teach me. I loved the smell of the wooden blocks and the new crayons. She fed me yogurt, wheat germ, and other healthy foods. She cared about my education and my nutrition. Mom told me to trust in God and Jesus. She pointed out the words "In God We Trust" on a dollar bill and took me to church, where I learned about God, Jesus, and the Bible in Sunday school.

My parents had a garden in the back yard. One time, I ran outside of the house buck naked and streaked through the garden in an exhilarating run of toddler freedom. I remember terrible fights between my mother and father. They rolled on the floor in a fistfight. My father restrained my mother on the floor, and she screamed to me, "Go get the butcher knife." I froze. I could not get a knife to kill my father. It was a terrible memory. After that, I played outside with my younger brother. We seemed to be in the way, inside. Perhaps my mother was trying to create space between us to protect us from her rapidly deteriorating mind and violent delusions.

My father realized that his wife was slipping mentally. She wanted to move to Pensacola, Florida, to be near her parents, who had a pecan tree orchard and farm. We visited the farm and then moved a few miles away. My parents started having more severe marital problems.

My father was a traveling salesman and was gone on long trips for months at a time. My mother thought, in her delusional state, he was having an affair. So he moved out. The possible postpartum depression or psychosis she experienced became full-blown paranoid schizophrenia. She planned a delusional trip to Heaven. She went to the hardware store and purchased a gun. She sent my dad a bouquet of flowers as a sympathy remembrance to his mother's home in Philadelphia, where he lived. She put a sign in the window of our home that read: *Don't come in. I have a gun, and I will shoot my children.* She asked me at seven years old if I wanted to go to Heaven. I had been to Sunday school at the Church of Christ and knew Heaven was a wonderful place. I said, "Sure, if I can bring my dollies." She said I could take my dolls, and I agreed to go to Heaven with my mother. She gave my brother and me a full bottle of children's aspirins, laid us down on her bed, covered our ears with towels, and shot both of us three times. Then she shot herself in the head three times. The Lord's angels directed the bullets. I still have a bullet in my back that was too close to my spinal cord to remove. The bullets went in at an angle into my mother's head, and she survived as well. The Lord's mercy and grace was at work in the nanoseconds of those bullet blasts.

The next thing I remember is the hospital ER, where we were getting our stomachs pumped. Blood covered our clothes. We stayed in the hospital for a long time, and then we were taken to my maternal grandparents' home in Mobile, Alabama. I cried for my father as their car drove away from the hospital. My grandmother turned around and said she would beat me with a belt if I didn't stop crying for that horrible man I called my father.

Shortly after we arrived, our grandfather passed away. Our grandmother showed us no love or affection, only abuse and hate. My brother had epilepsy and had seizures all the time. Everyone and everything seemed bad to me as a young girl. Our grandmother would tell both my brother and me that we would go crazy just like our mother. We were conditioned to believe we were horrible and would at any moment become paranoid schizophrenics and hurt someone.

Although my father had initially attempted to get full custody of us and move us to his mother's home in Philadelphia, he was advised by psychologists that my mother would never recover if she felt her children had been moved away from her permanently. He decided to give up all parental rights to my brother and me when I was seven and my brother was five years old. He must have known from my mother how awful her childhood had been, hearing the horror stories about my grandmother. Yet he left us with our maternal grandmother, and our fate was to be tortured physically, emotionally, psychologically, and spiritually for the rest of our time at her home.

My grandmother got tired of looking at us, so she packed us up and sent us to the Church of Christ, Childhaven Orphanage in Cullman, Alabama. It was an orphanage, but I loved being there. They took us to church every Sunday. It was there, as an orphan neglected by her family and all alone, that I received Christ as my Savior. The Holy Spirit wanted me all to Himself.

The Lord became both my loving Mother and Father. My heavenly Father would never give up His rights to be my Father. I cherished my time spent at church and in prayer. My relationship with Jesus was very important to me.

I wrote to one of my mother's sisters about the fun times I was having at the orphanage. My aunt mentioned to my grandmother that she was glad I was having fun and was able to be with children my own age in the small home assigned to my age group at the orphanage. For some reason, this information enraged my grandmother, and she immediately made plans to shuttle me back to her home in Mobile, leaving me to be tortured instead of letting me live in a positive environment. She spoke about me in derogatory terms to everyone in our family. Apparently, I was the cause of her heart problems and diabetes, my mother's problems, and my brother's epilepsy. She hated me with a passion and lied about me to everyone. I knew. I heard her say these things on the phone.

The only respite was the times spent at the orphanage. At least there, I didn't have to listen to her diatribe about how horrible her grandchild was. My times at the orphanage were sunshine to me. I enjoyed washing dishes after meals in the big institutional kitchen. I received praise because I loaded and unloaded the industrial dishwasher at an incredible speed. I had friends. We went to the movies and to the roller skating rink. It was awesome. We celebrated birthdays and holidays and baked cookies in the homes we lived in. No one abused me or was mean to me. I wore the clothes I wanted to look nice and I did my hair in pretty styles. No one shouted and screamed at me that I was horrible and nothing.

I learned to use reverse psychology on my grandmother and begged her not to send me back to the orphanage. I knew she would send me back if she thought I did not want to go, and of course, she did. One of the last times I was there, I even dated someone. All the times at the orphanage were used by the Lord to show me that life could be good and somewhat normal, and He was always there to help me, even when my life was in constant chaos.

When I was fourteen, my grandmother dropped me off in the parking lot of a local shopping center and said to get a job or don't come home. She said she was tired of paying for my food and clothes. I'm sure she knew that the current Alabama law for minors to obtain a job was fifteen years old. After being turned down by several businesses when I said I was fourteen, I wound up at a Baskin Robbins ice cream shop. Mrs. Stuckey, the kind owner, asked how old I was. I was always tall for my age, so when I said fifteen, she said, "You're hired." She gave me a short-sleeved brown-striped uniform and hat. As I walked home from my new job, I realized that I still had a home to go to that night. My grandmother took all the checks I earned and used the money for herself. I never saw a dime of it.

I didn't know it at the time, but my grandmother had been receiving social security benefits for my brother and me. She didn't need the money I made at my little part-time job. She had falsified my birth certificate to say that she was my birth mother and left the father's name blank. She "legally" adopted me with this birth certificate. In an act of psychological warfare, she tried to erase every good memory of my father in my mind. As an adult, I refused to participate in this lie. On my children's birth certificates, I used my real biological family name from my original birth certificate.

One day, Mrs. Stuckey noticed scratch marks on my arms and neck when I came into work. She asked if I was abused at home. I told her that I was. I had tried to get help at my high school, but no one believed me. CPS had visited our home after a relative reported my grandmother for abuse, but they didn't do anything. I was relieved that someone cared enough to believe me. Mrs. Stuckey called the police. I climbed up on top of the walk-in freezer at Baskin Robbins and hid behind boxes just in case my grandmother came storming in before the police arrived. I was placed in St. Mary's Shelter for Girls and later transitioned to the St. Mary's Girls Home by St. Ann's Catholic Church in downtown Mobile, which is still there today. The horrible abuse was over, but I regretted leaving my brother in that house with our grandmother. Before I left, I asked him if he wanted to go with me. He asked if I knew for sure I would get away with leaving. When I said I didn't know, he chose to stay there. Unfortunately, CPS didn't remove him from that abusive home.

The administrator at the girls' home was Mary Waldrup, a tough old gal who was former military and smoked unfiltered Camel cigarettes. Ms. Mary was kind to me. My saving grace at the time was my first cousin Linda and her husband, Danny. They found out I was living in the orphanage and arranged with Ms. Mary to take me on weekend outings. I am so thankful to them for their kindnesses at the most difficult time of my life as a young girl.

Linda helped place an ad in a Philadelphia paper about me and asked that my father, Allen Zesewitz, contact her. Someone saw the ad and contacted my dad. He arranged with the girls' home to see me. When he visited, he asked me to move to Philadelphia, but I was dating a boy and loved my new life. I was about to graduate from high school and go to business college, so I decided not to move. However, I visited him and his family several times and enjoyed the beautiful snow for the holidays. I met my Uncle John, Aunt Elaine, my teenage cousins Mark and Paul, and other relatives I never knew I had. It was a long-distance relationship, but I had a father who wasn't anything like my grandmother had described. She told me he was a rotten person, and I should always hate him. Her evil demands failed. The Lord won my heart, and I still have a close relationship with my dad, who is now retired and lives in Florida.

In my early twenties, I ignored the fact that my mother was mentally ill. I said she had passed away, even though she had lived most of her life in a mental asylum or was homeless. On one of her trips back to Mobile, she contacted me. I was in college at the time, active in a Baptist church in children's ministry, and I worked a part-time job at the Corps of Engineers. I wanted her to live with me and for us to be a family again. She stayed with me for several weeks, and then one day, she disappeared. I heard from a relative that she was seen on the streets in California—a homeless, mentally ill person. It was hard for me to understand. She died many years later from lung cancer in the Searcy Hospital mental asylum.

After my mother left me again, I managed to finish business college and was hired as an administrative assistant at Brookley Field Air Force Base in Mobile, Alabama—the same place where my parents had met. At the time, I did not realize I was repeating my mother's history.

I then moved to Texas and worked as a training coordinator for the Department of Treasury Office of Thrift Supervision. I married and we started our family. Two years later my husband passed away suddenly, and I became a young widow.

The Lord got my attention in earnest. I relied on the Lord God to be my husband and to be Father to my children. I was drawn to the Lord on a deeper level through women's Bible study and being a church volunteer and Christian preschool teacher at our church's Mother's Day Out program. The Holy Spirit began to do a work in my heart, soul, and mind. I threw myself into my Savior's arms, and He caught me, even though I tried to reconstruct my life on my own terms by remarriage to someone who turned out to be a physical abuser. Once I found out that the abuse I had suffered from my childhood had conditioned me to accept abuse, for the sake of my children I immediately prayed to the Lord to find the courage to be functional instead of dysfunctional. I ended any opportunity for future abuse of my children or myself. I refused to accept abuse as a norm. I wanted more for my family. My Savior never left me and helped me finally adopt healthy boundaries.

I was a single-parent Christian mom for many years. I served the Lord in various church ministries, and my children were raised in the church. The Lord's desires became the desires of my heart. I desired a loving Christian home. I desired to be married to a godly spiritual leader who would be a good father to my children. I desired a peaceful home and family and service to the Lord in ministry. I never expected the mysterious twist the Lord would bring my way.

I met my husband at church. He asked me to marry him at our church, and we were married there with our children at our sides. The Lord took what the Evil One was sure he had destroyed, and God renewed, reconciled, and restored my life. We attended a Blended Family Course and Pre-Marital Counseling before we were married. The Lord was reconstructing Debra into the godly wife and mother I had always desired to be. Having a blended family was more difficult than we ever thought it would be. Each of our children had been half orphaned and experienced varying degrees of early childhood trauma. At times, we were not sure how we would get through the next traumatic experience.

Then the Lord gave me a class called Family to Family, by the National Association of Mental Illness (NAMI). One of our children began to act out at home, and it reminded me of something I wanted to forget—mental illness. I went to the class and learned that mental illness is a biological condition that affects the brain. I taught classes for the next eight years and helped over 500 families with loved ones who had severe mental illness. My husband and I appeared on television to discuss properly dealing with a loved one's mental illness.

The Lord opened up the world of mental illness difficulty to me and helped our family. It was a cathartic experience. I understood what my mother had gone through. She had postpartum psychosis. It was not diagnosed, counseled, or medicated. It turned into paranoid schizophrenia, which was also undiagnosed or medicated.

I called my husband after my first class of Family to Family at Argosy University in Dallas and told him that these people understood what we were going through in the privacy of our home. They had practical advice and offered hope to effectively deal with our loved ones who were struggling with mental illness and addiction. I called my brother in Alabama and asked if he remembered our grandmother always saying we would go crazy like our mom. He said he did remember. I said that was not going to happen. I had been educated on mental illness, and I now realized that we would be all right.

Our mother had spiraled into attempted murder and suicide because no one gave her proper mental health care. I forgave her, because she was not responsible for her tragic actions. The Holy Spirit changed my heart and mind. I don't have any bad feelings toward her anymore. The Holy Spirit also healed my heart regarding my father. He was a young, inexperienced man who was overwhelmed by his wife's mental illness. He did not know what to do, so he did nothing. He could not possibly know what he didn't know. It was a tragic situation for him as well—one that almost destroyed his own sanity and rendered him paralyzed as a human being.

After my cathartic healing, the Lord was so gracious. Now at fifty-five years old, I do love my mother and father. I realize that in my mother's case, the mental health condition she had was genetic. My grandmother also suffered from schizophrenia. I have come to realize the positive things my grandmother did for me: she taught me how to take care of a home, maintain appropriate landscaping, and how to cook and clean. She gave me an example of how to manage a family and a budget. I am grateful to her for taking care of me in the only way she knew how, albeit extremely dysfunctional. I am personally proud of the work the Lord has done in my heart and soul to break the dysfunctional cycle with my own family. Each of my loving Christian family members have made decisions to ask Jesus into their hearts and have been baptized. We have a loving Christian family.

One of my mother's brothers and my brother had been going to visit my mother at the asylum, sometimes taking her home for the weekend. There are photos of them sitting on the front porch of their home, relaxing and being a family. I am indebted to my uncle and brother for showing her such compassion in her last days on this earth. My uncle called to inform me that my mother had passed away, and I made plans to attend her funeral. However, one of my children started running a fever and I had to stay home. I know my mother is in Heaven now. All her mental illness is healed, and she is happy, healthy, and mentally stable, cradled in the arms of Jesus. Her mental turmoil is over.

My near-death experience has been used by the Lord to humble me. Instead of hiding the fact that my mother was mentally ill, I reveal it when my testimony can help someone. Once I realized how devastating mental illness could be, I knew I couldn't blame her or hate her anymore. Heavenly Father God, Jesus, and the Holy Spirit have worked to educate me about mental health. I have been able to help many families understand and forgive their mentally ill loved ones.

The Lord took my greatest sadness and turned it into His ministry to others. My greatest ministry came from my deepest pain of having a traumatic childhood. The fact that I am alive today and have been able to walk is a miracle of the Lord. I realize that my life purpose is to help others who are walking through the pain of domestic violence and mental illness. There is hope, and His name is Jesus Christ. As a young girl, I asked Jesus into my heart as my Savior. He put all the broken pieces of my heart back together and healed me of early childhood trauma, neglect, psychological and physical abuse, bitterness, unforgiveness, and anger. If my heavenly Father and His Son Jesus can heal me, anyone can be healed. Your healing and peace is God's miracle just waiting to happen. Ask Him into your heart today. You will be amazed at how different your life can become. Your restoration is waiting.

Debra Moore *is a loving Christian wife and mother of wonderful adult children and one spoiled grand dog, DJ. Mental health training and family education is her passion. Debra's heart for the mentally ill comes from having had a mother with severe mental health difficulties. She is a political advocate for Mental Health Reform in Texas before the Texas Legislature. Debra was featured on the Wake-Up Radio Show with the Comish and interviewed by CBS 11 Reporter Russ McCaskey for Mental Health Month. She is a National Alliance on Mental Illness (NAMI) North Texas Family-to-Family instructor and has helped over 500 families with their mentally ill loved ones. Please contact her at* **PatrickMooresWife@yahoo.com** *or* **972.513.3086.**

Thoughts to Ponder
from Mental Illness and a Near-Miss Bullet

1. God is there to help, even when your life is in chaos.

2. The Lord can take what the evil one thought he destroyed and renew, reconcile, and restore it.

3. God can help you develop healthy boundaries.

How can you help someone who has poor mental health?

The thief comes only to steal and kill and destroy;
I have come that they may have life,
and have it to the full. — John 10:10

Standing before the Mirror
by Majeedah Murad

My name means *glorious*. When I was a little girl, my parents told me that Majeedah, or ماجده written in Arabic, meant "noble and generous." They were right. Majeedah means all these things. When people meet me, they often ask about my name, followed by questions about my ethnicity and parents' nationalities. My father is a Black or African American from the South. My mother was a Black West-Indian from Trinidad. They met in Brooklyn, New York.

In the late 1960s and early 1970s, the Nation of Islam was widely popular with Black people in the northeast United States. The message of Black nationalism espoused by Elijah Muhammad appealed to African Americans who were watching the battle for civil rights unfold in the South.

My parents joined the Nation of Islam with many of their relatives and friends. After becoming Muslims, they legally changed our names to Arabic names. But I have always been Majeedah Murad. No middle name, just Majeedah—the glorious one. My testimony is one of overcoming numerous obstacles, relinquishing my rights, and walking with Jesus as Savior and Lord.

In 1981 my family moved from Brooklyn, New York, to North Port, Florida. We might as well have moved to Alaska. Talk about culture shock. We were living in the boondocks, complete with insects, reptiles, and trees for miles and miles. We went from the comfort of being surrounded by people who were racially and religiously like us, to becoming the only Black family on the block, and probably the only Muslims in the entire city. Without question, moving from Brooklyn to North Port dramatically changed the course of my life. In some ways, I will forever be grateful, but in other ways, I still fight to overcome.

My earliest memories are of attending *madrassa* (school in Arabic) and worshiping at the mosque with my family. I cannot recall a time when I didn't believe in the existence of God—or as I used to call him, Allah (God in Arabic). I stood before the bathroom mirror asking Allah, "Why am I here? What do you want me to do with my life?" Why I was asking God about the purpose of my existence as an eight-year-old eludes me. God Himself must have put that question into my mind. Hebrews 11:6 says, "And without faith it is impossible to please God, because anyone who comes to Him must believe that He exists and that He rewards those who earnestly seek Him." I had never heard these words, yet as a little girl, I believed in God's existence and was earnestly seeking Him. Decades later, seeking God led me to become a missionary with Wycliffe Bible Translators.

My parents divorced when I was ten. Life changed in unimaginable ways. I was confused and numb. Before the divorce, we were not wealthy, but I never felt poor. My father drove new cars. We lived in a house on a corner lot with a big back yard, swing set, and orange trees. We played outside, rode our bikes, and on weekends went to the beach for family outings. There was always enough to eat. I was, for the most part, a carefree little girl whose biggest problem was protecting my Hello Kitty from being attacked by my siblings. After the divorce, my father visited a handful of times until he stopped visiting altogether. I did not see him again until I was in my early twenties with a child of my own. I felt abandoned and didn't want to be a financial burden on my mother, who was already suffering.

In the intervening years, my siblings and I assumed the role my father refused to fill, by working to provide for our household. Although I became an adult far too quickly, I now appreciate how God used my childhood for good. I developed character traits that enabled me to graduate from law school while working and parenting a toddler as a single mother.

In January 2000, I began studying at the University of Florida Levin College of Law. My son was twenty-two months old. All first-year law students take the same courses. Torts began promptly at 9:00 a.m., but daycare did not open until 8:30 a.m. By the time I dropped my son off, drove to law school, and hunted for a parking spot, class had already begun. My tardiness became a pattern. I was so embarrassed. Every day I slinked into the classroom and took my seat in the back row. One day, my neighbor made a snarky comment about my tardiness when I asked him a question. To his credit, he later apologized, but my feelings of embarrassment—and worse yet, feelings of shame—only grew.

In addition to the tardiness, I amassed an impressive collection of parking tickets. I was indignant. Being late to class every day was bad enough. I didn't need to be greeted by a parking ticket afterward. Besides, I had no money to pay for the tickets. So I devised a clever solution. I shoved an old parking ticket under the driver-side windshield wiper before going to class. It worked brilliantly—sometimes. As a first-year law student, I already had the makings of a shrewd lawyer.

Law school was an extremely challenging time. Reading hundreds of pages every night was rigorous, and grades were determined by one exam. Money was tight, so tight that I sought permission from the Dean of Students to work—something first-year law students are expressly forbidden to do. The dean granted my request. Because he was such a kind man, he offered me a personal loan, which I was too proud to accept. My childhood taught me that everything was up to me. I had to be self-sufficient. I couldn't burden anybody else with my problems. My glory was in pulling myself up by my bootstraps. There was no grace. There was no mercy. My job was to keep my world on its axis and be perfect while balancing the weight. If only I had known about the God, Who daily bears our burdens.

During my second year of law, my mother suffered a massive stroke and school life became even more challenging. She was completely paralyzed on one side and barely able to mumble a few words. My siblings and I moved her to a nursing home in Gainesville, where I attended law school. To my surprise, she became a gentler woman after the stroke. She even possessed a *sweetness*, a word I never would have used to describe my mom.

My weeks consisted of going to class, studying, parenting, exercising, and visiting my mom as often as possible. Despite the incredible difficulty of that season, I am grateful for the time we spent together. I graduated from law school in December 2002, on schedule with the rest of my class. In her wheelchair, my mother attended my graduation, beaming with pride.

After graduating, I was asked by my son's daycare to leave

because I was no longer a student. While preparing for the bar exam and working a full-time job, I now had to find another daycare. The Montessori school we visited was too expensive. But just down the road, a Christian daycare was within my meager budget. Shortly after he was enrolled, my son told me about baby Jesus and insisted that we bless our food before eating. Without realizing the true significance of what he was doing, I thought, *That's so cute.* Isaiah 11:6 says, "The wolf will live with the lamb, the leopard will lie down with the goat, the calf and the lion and the yearling together; and a little child will lead them." Surely, my little five-year-old was leading me.

From my third year of law school, I worked as a law clerk at the Alachua County attorney's office. I was overjoyed when the county attorney offered me a permanent position. I could remain in Gainesville and not have to move my mother. Several months later, a law school classmate and friend, who also lived in Gainesville, invited me and my son to her parents' home for dinner. Her parents, Ralph and Mary Coryell, had lived in Gainesville for years, but oddly enough, we had never met. That night, Mary invited me to something called Alpha. I don't know why I said yes. There was something different about this lady. Mary was winsome and barely knew me. I sensed her sincerity, and she adored my son.

Through Alpha, I explored Christianity and a man named Jesus. His claims of exclusivity seemed preposterous. After all, I was a good person living in a world of similarly good people—more or less. And even if I was a bad person, according to His pejorative standard, didn't I deserve a pass due to the hardships I had endured? How could He be the one true God? What did that mean for everybody else? What arrogance.

I would still be asking these questions today if my mother had not died. On May 7, 2004, two days before Mother's Day, she passed away. My grief caused me to deeply contemplate the meaning of life. What was the point of this seemingly endless cycle of suffering and hardship? At twenty-eight, I became that eight-year-old girl again, standing before the mirror, talking to God, Whom I now believed to be capricious and cruel.

Over the next several months, God slowly softened my heart. I needed the hope Jesus offered. I needed to know someone

109

who would never leave me and loved me unconditionally. Psalm 27:10 says, "Though my father and mother forsake me, the Lord will receive me." And He did. On my twenty-ninth birthday, I became a follower of Jesus during an Alpha retreat. Ralph and Mary were instrumental in my conversion. At the time, I did not realize how much they were praying for me. Not only did they pray, they adopted me and my son as members of their family.

One weekend, we all went for a walk. I told Ralph that everything looked different, more vibrant, more alive. It was as though I had removed a pair of glasses I no longer needed. For the first time, I saw clearly.

I became a lawyer to help people. I planned to become a social worker championing the rights of the poor and oppressed. My English professor, whose husband was a circuit court judge, convinced me I could do more for people as an attorney. Many days I wondered whether practicing law was making any difference in the world. Here I was, a responsible citizen, raising my son, and contributing to society. Was I doing what God wanted me to do? Was I helping anybody?

As a new Christian studying the Bible, I was awestruck by the things Jesus said and did. What did He mean in Matthew 16:25 when He said, "For whoever wants to save their life will lose it, but whoever loses their life for Me will find it." And what about Matthew 19:30? "But many who are first will be last, and many who are last will be first." And in Matthew 6:19–21, He said, "Do not store up for yourselves treasures on Earth, where moths and vermin destroy, and where thieves break in and steal. But store up for yourselves treasures in Heaven, where moths and vermin do not destroy, and where thieves do not break in and steal. For where your treasure is, there your heart will be also." Jesus' Kingdom appeared to be upside down in a confusing but bizarrely attractive way.

By Western standards, I am not a materialistic person. Anyone who knows me can vouch for this. For instance, I purchased a new car a few months before graduating from law school because the old one—the car I used to put the parking tickets on—finally gave out. I drove the new car for sixteen years before selling it in 2018. Money is important. I know firsthand that having money makes life so much easier.

However, my education was mine. Against insurmountable odds, I graduated from law school and passed the bar exam. I fully expected—better yet, I *deserved*—to reap the benefits of my hard work. Not just economically, but by my position in society.

Today, Black women earn 25 percent less than White men, and 6 percent less than White women. This disparity decreases with more education. Through my training as an attorney, I had the opportunity to level the playing field. Was it possible that Jesus required me to surrender for His sake what I worked so hard to achieve?

The plain-meaning rule is a legal principle that favors interpreting unambiguous language according to its ordinary and obvious meaning without analyzing legislative intent. As a lawyer reading Jesus' words, I could not escape the plain meaning of the red text. The answer to my question was yes, He could require me to surrender my career.

My journey of becoming a missionary started in 2010 when my church did a study by Henry Blackaby called *Experiencing God.* The premise is that God speaks today. He is always at work around us. He invites us to participate in His work. And invariably, His invitation will cause a crisis of belief.

I experienced my crisis of belief in March 2010, when God asked me to resign from my position as an Assistant County Attorney, go back to school, and study music. Although I had played the violin for many years, that sounded ridiculous. I prayed and fasted about it for weeks. God repeatedly confirmed His words, so I obeyed. Other than sensing that this transition involved worship, I had no earthly idea where it would lead.

In April 2011, I visited Texas to learn more about ministry through music. I attended a World Arts open house at the Graduate Institute of Applied Linguistics (now Dallas International University) in Dallas. World Arts combines arts with missions to evangelize unreached people groups. As I participated in one of the sessions one weekend, I realized with stunning clarity that God was asking me to become a missionary. Within three months, my son and I moved from Gainesville, Florida, to Duncanville, Texas. God provided a paralegal position at a bankruptcy law firm in downtown Dallas. John 21:25 says, "Jesus did many other things as well. If every one of them were written down, I suppose that even the whole world would not have room for the books that would be written." I relate to this passage.

Jesus did so many things over the next several years that I cannot share them all. He made connections I could not have made for myself. He redirected my steps—going before me and clearing the way. During this period, the Lord was teaching me about missions and healing my heart. I learned so much about walking closely with Him and how He could heal and redeem my past.

Over the years, my dialogue with God about missions remained open. He never said *no*, just *not yet*. I continued seeking direction and resumed practicing law with the bankruptcy firm. In 2018, when my son was a sophomore in college, I wondered again whether I should pursue missions. I asked this question with some trepidation. Frankly, I was comfortable. I had practiced bankruptcy law for four years and enjoyed it. After the massive transition in 2010 and the loss of earning potential and professional opportunities, I didn't want to embrace the changes associated with a missionary lifestyle. It seemed that making this leap of faith should be easier the second time. It wasn't. I again wrestled with the same questions as before. By God's grace, I reached the same answer. Yes, He could require me to surrender my career for His sake. After some investigation, I learned that Wycliffe Bible Translators had a tremendous need for attorneys. This was not a paid position. I had to raise my financial support just like any other missionary. However, it was possible for me to serve God with the skills I already had as a missionary and an attorney, a missionary attorney helping people.

On August 1, 2019, after much prayer and discernment, I joined Wycliffe Bible Translators USA as Associate General Counsel.

Wycliffe has more than 3,000 employees serving around the world to share the gospel of Jesus Christ through Bible translation. I began handling a variety of Wycliffe's legal issues such as contracts, employment, tax, insurance, real estate, non-patent intellectual property, international law, and more.

My testimony is one of God's prevenient grace. Throughout my life, long before I accepted Him as Savior, Jesus showered

His extravagant love upon me in a way that has enabled me to walk with Him as Lord. Matthew 5:45 says, "He causes His sun to rise on the evil and the good, and sends rain on the righteous and the unrighteous." I have been evil. I have been unrighteous. But God has been faithful and true. As 2 Timothy 2:11–13 reminds us, "Here is a trustworthy saying: If we died with Him, we will also live with Him; if we endure, we will also reign with Him. If we disown Him, He will disown us; if we are faithless, He will remain faithful, for He cannot disown Himself." My name means *glorious*, and I have learned that all the glory belongs to God alone.

__Majeedah Murad__ is an attorney licensed to practice law in Florida and Texas. She began her career almost seventeen years ago as a local government lawyer in Florida. Most recently she practiced bankruptcy law with a firm in downtown Dallas. After feeling called toward missions for many years, in August 2019, Majeedah became a missionary with Wycliffe Bible Translators USA, serving as Associate General Counsel. Majeedah is excited about this opportunity to support Wycliffe's vision of ensuring that people from every language understand the Bible and experience transformation. To become a prayer partner in Majeedah's Wycliffe ministry, please visit
__https://www.Wycliffe.org/Partner/Murad.__
Contact her at __Majeedah_Murad@Wycliffe.org.__

Thoughts to Ponder
from Standing before the Mirror

1. God is sovereign. You make plans, and He directs your steps.

2. God heals, redeems, and uses your experiences for His valuable plan.

3. God rewards the sacrifice of your plans with something much better.

What have you surrendered to follow Jesus?

If we are faithless, he will remain faithful,
for he cannot disown himself. — 2 Timothy 2:13

Beautifully Molded
by Starlet Bell

From childhood until young adulthood, I lived "in-story." Sometimes, my dreams were varied and inviting as I found love within the storyline. Other times, I sat alone, daydreaming in the most peculiar places. My dreams were filled with adventure as well as occasional conflict, but the last part of my dreams was deeply absorbing and filled with relational love. I might have been the heroine in distress or the one stranded on a faraway island, but I was always rescued. Therefore, dreaming was one of my fun pastimes.

My favorite dream occurred when I was six years old. One evening, I went to bed afraid because my mother and father were shouting at each other. I shivered, because fear overwhelmed me. My older sister and I shared a full bed, so I wasn't alone, but after she fell asleep, I put her arm over my body for assurance.

That night, I cried myself to sleep, because my sister's "arm of assurance" wasn't helping. I awoke to a bright, shining light that came through my bedroom door and cascaded over the room. Immediately, I was frightened and pulled my covers up to my neck. I saw an outline of a body with two arms outstretched and an unidentifiable face. The figure was clothed in a white flowing gown that glittered. Nothing was said. Nothing happened—except I felt an overwhelming peace. I was not afraid but felt strong. I returned to deep sleep. When I awoke the next morning, I looked at the door and nothing was there—just a normal wooden white door with hinges. I questioned what I thought I had seen. I never knew for certain if it was real or a dream. However, this experience helped me later as I faced obstacles.

As a young girl, I kept many secrets in my dysfunctional home. Because of my insecurities, I felt extremely alone. I wanted approval from anyone I played or associated with. I was always walking on eggshells and looking behind me. *What shadow did I cast? How did people perceive me?* I did not feel "real" in my skin.

I daydreamed for hours on a park bench and studied people while eating a hamburger. I role-played in my mind what it would be like to live in their shoes. They looked so content and happy.

Even though I played with friends, they never knew my secret. They also didn't know my father like they knew my mother, because he worked late every night. He was preoccupied with the great outdoors, fishing, and enjoying spirited drinks.

Many nights I lay in bed crying and thinking, *Why wasn't I a boy instead of a girl? My father would be so happy with me if I were a boy, because I could go fishing with him. He might even find time to come to one of my birthday parties. Then he would hug me and tell me he loved me.* My father and I didn't get much time together before he died. I was seventeen when my hope of having a father/daughter relationship ended.

Unfortunately, it was years later when I came to a deeper understanding of God and how much He loved me just as I was, unconditionally. As I continued the path of approval-finding, I married someone who promised to care for me for the rest of my life. After living "in-story" for such a long time, I was excited about finally creating my own story. I believed that it would fill the hole in my heart.

However, the longevity of emotional and physical abuse by my spouse tore up my life and became "death blows." I was exhausted from crawling out windows and hiding from someone who had lost control. Alcohol and drugs were his priority. I believed I had nothing to offer and felt purposeless.

One night after my husband crazily approached me wielding a butcher knife, I asked God to "please take me," because I was tired of the abuse and wanted to permanently escape. I shouldn't have lived through that night, but for some reason, my husband dropped the butcher knife and ran from me. This was a mystery to me. God spared my life and revealed His miracle of mercy and grace. After this event, I took steps to understand with my whole heart my Father's miracle of kindness and forgiveness.

It didn't stay this way forever. My fears of a worst-case scenario happened. Late one evening, I received a telephone call from a woman I could hardly understand. She was sobbing, and her voice was muffled.

I said, "Who is this? What is wrong?"

She regained her composure and shared that she and my spouse had been having an affair for some time. A feeling of death came over me. I became severely depressed and lost an extreme amount of weight.

I was exhausted from running. When I swept my kitchen floor, I swept up mounds of hair that had fallen out. My countenance did not look like my former self. I was in despair and no longer thought life was worth living. However, God intervened. I went to a hospital where I began to heal inside and outside. It was a safe place where I felt loved and cared for.

I found a Bible in the drawer by my bed. The scriptures I read began to "pop" off the pages. There were words such as hope, faith, and courage that stuck in my heart. It was there that God rocked me, loved me, and told me I was molded in His image and that His DNA was woven into me. All the things my Sunday school teachers had taught me were coming back to life. God showed me that I was given His authority over anyone and anything.

In that hospital room, I experienced a shift in my consciousness that would forever change my life. I realized that I had been separated from God, because I had idolized man above God and looked for my security through man. I asked Jesus to come into my life, forgive my sin, and take out the darkness inside of me. This was where my newfound relationship with God began. That was where I bowed in wonder and spoke out the words, "More . . . I want more of You." I knew I was clothed in righteousness and radiant in His perfect love. I was beautifully molded.

I finally approached the thought of getting a divorce. The word "divorce" was such a foreign word to me, because I had taken wedding vows "to have and to hold until death do us part." After wise counsel from two credible people, I filed and started moving forward toward a new life. Several days before the divorce was final, I was outside in a church parking lot, intensely discussing my marriage with a dear friend. I knew the divorce needed to happen, but I was shaky and felt wary of that dreaded day.

Out of the blue, something incredible happened. Toward the end of our talk, I looked up at the beautiful sky that God had created with His own hands, and I saw something small drifting down from the sky. I thought it was a small piece of paper. The opening where we were standing had no tree limbs above it and there were no signs of a bird nearby. For some reason, I extended my open hand and soon found a beautiful, white furry feather lying in my palm. This feather was not large, but for some wonderful reason, I had caught it in mid-air.

My friend and I were shocked to witness something so meaningful and profound. In the past two months, I had found feathers in peculiar places such as the bathroom stall at work, on the copier, on my desk, and in my car. Anytime I found them, I felt an extreme closeness to God, and I felt He continued to give me encouragement, boldness, and peace through the feathers He sent.

Because these feathers were of different shapes, sizes, and appearances, I felt they each meant something a little different. It is still a mystery to me, but I choose to believe that they could have been feathers sent from Heaven. Psalm 91:4 came to mind: "He will cover you with His feathers, and under His wings you will find refuge; His faithfulness will be your shield and rampart." I pray this scripture daily.

Today, I not only like myself, but I love myself unconditionally. God has taught me to look at the *hearts* of people and not their faces. God promised me plans for a beautiful future, and when He makes a promise, He keeps His promise. I can't adequately express how different my life is today. I no longer suffer from insecurities. I am at peace, and I love unconditionally. I am a bolder person, because I know who I am in Christ.

My life has been stable. I have worked for thirty years as an educator and principal, and for the last ten years, I have run my own company. I work with pastors and churches as a leadership and grief coach. My love for life has always been about children, and I have been blessed to work with at-risk students who lived in dysfunctional homes. I encourage them to "speak" the truth of Jesus in their little minds and hearts. On the day of my retirement as a principal, I was blessed to have my students present gifts and call me their "praying principal." I recently became a Stonecroft speaker, where I continue to spread the Word of Jesus in all places.

Several years after my divorce, I received a wonderful gift from God—a Christian husband. He rode in on a white horse, but he didn't have to rescue me, because God had already rescued me. It was a romance story filled with love as well as obedience and faith in our Father. We met on a Sunday at the church coffee pot in the foyer. There was a connection at first sight. We dated, fell in love, and were married within two months. The prayer room of our church is where my husband asked God for His approval to marry me. This was a magical time in my life, and after eighteen years, remains magical. I finally get to live in my own story.

Another huge gift from God was the gift of forgiveness. I finally forgave my earthly father. I was angry with him for many years, because he never verbally expressed his love to me, and he was never there when I needed him. Pictures are worth a thousand words. God allowed my mother to retrieve a special picture of my dad and me. It showed my father holding a thirty-five-pound catfish in one hand and my small hand with his in the other. My mother explained that it was my two-year birthday, and I was dressed in birthday attire. She also explained that my father gave me my birth certificate name after he pondered it for five days. That picture and the one genuine conversation with my mother revealed that he did love me. I realized that under the circumstances, he did the best he could. I was finally able to forgive my father.

I experienced another blessing when I was able to forgive my ex-husband. Several years after the divorce, I picked up the phone and talked to him. As soon as I opened my mouth and let the words flow out, peace overtook me. It wasn't hard at all. God is a great big God, and not only did I apologize, but he apologized for all he had done. The greatest thing he apologized for was the incident with the butcher knife. When he did this, I asked him, "Why did you drop the knife?" He became very quiet and stammered. Then he said, "Because it became very, very hot. It almost burned my hand." That is when a huge change in him began. Today, he is sober and reading the Bible.

Through all these experiences of self-suffering, some induced by me, and some induced by others, I have learned more life lessons. I no longer idolize man but keep God at the top. Today I truly value my self-worth. I have a true relationship with God. Finally, I know I am not perfect, but I continue to live in "my story," the story of truth.

Starlet Bell is a Stonecroft Ministries' speaker who wants to lead dysfunctional, broken women to salvation. She is the creator of Shining Stars Coaching, where she serves as a Professional Leadership Coach to pastors and churches, locally and internationally. Starlet also does grief coaching. She is actively involved in Bible studies, speaking, and women's ministry. As an educator for thirty years and a principal for twelve years, the children loved her and nicknamed her the "Praying Principal." Starlet has authored two articles for major educational magazines in Texas. She and her husband have five children and fourteen grandchildren. E-mail her at StarletBell@suddenlink.net.

Thoughts to Ponder

from Beautifully Molded

1. God does not want you to keep harmful secrets.

2. You should not idolize people above God.

3. You are molded into God's image. His DNA is woven into you.

**What is your next step
toward better relationships?**

---

*He will cover you with His feathers,
and under His wings you will find refuge. — Psalm 91:4*

Hewn from an Ozark Rock

by Mark Tohlen

The psalmist declared, "Let the redeemed of the Lord tell their story." This is my story.

I was blessed to have been raised in a godly home surrounded by parents who loved the Lord. At the time, I did not think of my beginnings as humble, but by today's standards, we were not "encumbered" by great wealth. We were poor—yet we had all we needed. Soon after the Civil War, my mother's family arrived in the Ozarks. My dad's family was Swedish, immigrating to the heart of the Ozark's iron country in Dent County, Missouri, in 1888. My mother was born in a log cabin in Texas County, Missouri.

Thanks to my deep roots there, I understand and speak Ozark. The Ozark culture is strong, independent, and hardworking. There is a richness in the Ozark hills that is in my blood. The Ozark hills roll and swallow land including families, farms, and communities. To paraphrase the prophet, "I was hewn from these rocks" (Isaiah 51:1).

Times were tough, but that didn't stop us from having fun. My maternal grandpa loved to dance a jig while listening to the Grand Ole Opry on the huge console radio that loomed in the corner of his otherwise plain and simple home. My mom's family had many self-taught musicians. I loved hearing them play the piano, pump organ, fiddle, and electric organ while folks sang along. It was a little slice of Heaven right there in our home.

My dad built cooling towers for factories, which involved multiple, sophisticated systems. He was the combination of a skilled carpenter, metal worker, and water system expert. Dad could fix anything, which he had to do, because there was no money to buy new things.

I was the middle child of five boys who always found ways to have fun, both at home in St. Louis and during weekends on the Ozark farm. Video games? Who needs them when you have the wide-open land of the Ozarks to enjoy? We constantly explored, wrestled, hiked, climbed trees, caught frogs and snakes, and gave

Mom and Dad fits with all our rambunctiousness. Four of us older brothers shared two twin beds. My older brother, with whom I shared a bed, made me sleep with my face at his feet, saying my breath was awful. He was twice my size, so I did what I was told. But then he said my feet smelled. Sometimes when growing up, you just can't win.

When I was eight years old, I had a profound sense of my lostness. Though both my parents loved the Lord and took us to church every Sunday, my mom was the spiritual leader in our home. Listening to our pastor's sermons about Heaven and Hell, I felt the need to get saved. So I went to my mom and shared the burden of my little soul. She listened carefully, then told me she thought I was too young to make such a big decision. When I persisted, she took me to our pastor's house on a Saturday afternoon. The pastor asked me lots of questions and encouraged me to pray, then sent me back home with Mom.

The "hound of Heaven" was after me, and my desire to be saved persisted. Mom took me back to the pastor's house the next Saturday and this time, after another long conversation, we emerged from his parlor and into the living room where my mom was waiting.

"He's ready," the pastor said.

That was all I needed to hear. I decided to accept Christ as my Savior that day and was baptized later that month. I experienced joy and peace that I had never felt before, and that has stayed with me to this day.

I soon learned, however, that following Christ is not always easy. Because we didn't have a lot of money, there weren't a lot of Bibles in our home—they were too expensive. I developed a fondness for reading the Bible, so I borrowed my older brother's Bible and carried it with me every day from junior high through high school. Whenever I finished my school work in class, I opened his Bible and read until the bell rang at the end of class. Only a few of my classmates appreciated my Bible reading, and some made fun of me. This would not be the first time I faced resistance, even criticism, for my faith, but I believe those early experiences strengthened my commitment to the Lord.

When I read the Bible in school, I wasn't trying to offend

anyone or come off as "holier than thou." This ancient text came alive to me when I read it. How else can I explain the way the passages flashed into my mind and heart like a neon sign? I was, and still am, like the deer panting for water.

Time just slips away when I read the Bible. My daily experiences with reading the Bible prove to me how good God is. I am following the scent of the holy, and the trail leads through the Bible. Jesus is the central character of the Bible and everything points to Him. What a delightful companion for this journey.

I also love the way I can relate to the stories in the Bible. For example, Jesus learned carpentry skills from his earthly father, Joseph. I imagine the two of them in Joseph's carpentry shop. Surely Joseph took time to show Jesus all the secrets of being an excellent craftsman.

Similarly, my dad taught me the right way to work—how to use his carpentry and metal-working tools. In those conversations between a father and son, we also learned lessons about life. When Jesus said, "I am the way, the truth, and the life" (John 16:6), I heard him teaching me how to work for my heavenly Father here on Earth, right now. Everything that Jesus taught is there for me to apply to how I live today. For me, doing life "on Earth as it is in Heaven" (Mathew 6:10) changes how I relate to God first and then to others.

Throughout my journey as a Christian, I have been blessed with numerous people and resources that strengthened my faith. For example, there was Rev. H. Dale Jackson, my spiritual father and the pastor at our church during my teenage years. His son and I were best friends, and I spent a lot of time in their home. I loved that I could ask Pastor Jackson about anything. With him, there were no stupid questions. He always took my inquisitiveness seriously, which made a huge impact on me.

As a young adult, I did my best to please God, but I often failed to live up to His standards. Sometimes I experienced soaring spiritual highs. Other times I felt like the worst Christian around. Pastor Jackson helped me understand that this was a normal Christian experience. He taught me to take one day at a time and used the image of a ruler to help me see where I was yesterday and measure the change.

124

We may slip occasionally, but God can use that to help us grow. That's what sanctification is all about. Through the help of the Holy Spirit, we can grow each day, despite the mistakes we make. That was such a comfort to me.

By nature, I'm analytical and rely on logical thinking patterns. In addition to the Bible and Pastor Jackson, I have been guided on my journey by great Christian writers. For example, I believed in Satan but did not believe in demons. My logical mind just couldn't reconcile the two. Then I read *Mere Christianity* and *The Screwtape Letters* by C. S. Lewis. They, along with Scripture, helped me see that there must be demons, because Jesus cast them out easily. He couldn't get rid of something that didn't exist, right? "If I drive out demons by the finger of God, then the Kingdom of God has come upon you" (Luke 11:20). This may seem like a small matter, but it helped me as a father. Realizing that my innocent young children were vulnerable to outside forces, I prayed a wall of protection around our home.

I have also benefitted from the wisdom and encouragement of my four brothers. Jesus often spoke about how we are like brothers and sisters in a family, and it is indeed wonderful to be part of His great family of believers. But I'm also grateful that all four of my brothers are Christians. What a great privilege to walk the journey of faith with them.

Speaking of family, as a child, I so enjoyed the way my mom read the Bible to us. With my children, I tried to do the same but added the wonderful stories from *The Chronicles of Narnia*. Every night, I not only read the stories to our children—two boys and two girls—but also adopted the characters' voices. When we traveled to the one-room schoolhouse on our property in Dent County, Missouri, I built a fire on the old jacketed King stove and read all the Narnia stories to the kids. These readings are some highlights of joy in my life, and I believe they helped influence my children toward the faith. Thankfully, all four of our children were baptized in a cold, clear Ozark river by my preacher brother. The Methodist baptism ritual includes the line, "remember your baptism." My children will never forget their baptism—they nearly froze to death.

Although my walk with the Lord has produced great joy, it

has not been without its challenges. For example, Jesus tells us not to worry (Matthew 6:25), but I confess that I still do from time to time. My experience is that God prunes away what is not useful to His Kingdom. The understanding of sanctification that I learned from Pastor Jackson is comforting and helpful. For me, this living for Jesus can be tough. Jesus said the path is hard, but His yoke is easy (Matthew 11:30). My life's chaff and stubble, no matter how precious to me, are being burned. The Father's pruning reflects what is written in Hebrews 12:29, "our God is a consuming fire." With the Holy Spirit's help, I daily choose to live for Jesus and die to self.

As I began my career as an engineer, I soon learned that living by God's values required me to make some difficult decisions. For example, there were times when I was forced to choose between doing what was right in God's eyes or going along with what my boss or colleagues were doing. Whenever I took a stand for what was right, some of the people I worked with criticized me and tried to make me feel as if I wasn't a team player.

I have learned in the Bible that if we follow Christ, we will be persecuted. When it happens, it can be daunting. At the same time, however, taking a stand for what you believe ultimately brings great joy. Jesus said we would be blessed—which means made joyful—when we are persecuted because of righteousness (Matthew 5:10–12). From my own experience, I have learned just how true that is.

Throughout my journey of faith, God's Word has remained a constant and reliable guide. It is a living book that opens my imagination to a living God. Though its words appear as black-and-white images, they sparkle with all the vibrant colors of the rainbow. My imagination is reborn in the Trinity—three persons in one: God as a Father, Who providentially cares for me; Jesus, God's Son and my brother, in Whom I placed my faith as an eight-year-old; and the Holy Spirit, Who comforts and empowers me to live out my faith.

I learn from the Bible that grace is God acting before us and without our merit. The Old Testament is full of grace. The Exodus story is a story of grace. John in his gospel says that "grace and truth came through Jesus Christ" (John 1:17). "For

126

God so loved the world, that He gave His one and only Son" (John 3:16) is an act of grace. There is no other religion like this.

C. S. Lewis says, "There is a big story out there." The story is that Adam was made in perfection. Adam sinned, and we all fell. Jesus humbled Himself and came to show us what a perfect life looks like in submission to His Father. Jesus the Messiah was crucified, and three days later He walked out of the tomb just like His Father said He would. Jesus even told His disciples ahead of time that this was going to happen. There is no other story in the world like it. Praise God!

As I approach my senior years, I am more convinced of the goodness of God. He is a good Father, and I am grateful for the grace He has shown me, because I need it. Looking back, I can see all the times when, like the apostle Paul, "what I want to do I do not do, but what I hate I do" (Romans 7:15). No matter how hard I tried to do the right things, I made many mistakes.

For example, I never knew how challenging it was to be a father, and I regret the many missteps I made along the way. But because of God's grace, I know that I've been forgiven and given a clean slate. What a wonderful gift. As an analytical type, I never paid much attention to these heart issues, but reading John Bunyan's *Grace Abounding to the Chief of Sinners* helped me understand the reality of "heart mechanics." Life is filled with temptations, and sometimes we will fail. But God's grace picks us up, heals our scars, and sets us back on our way to walk with Him in victory.

I am a simple man, hewn from the rocks of the Ozarks. I was given the gift of faith at an early age, and God has blessed me in ways I could never imagine. Not everyone in the Ozarks has a family like mine that has been here for more than a hundred years. Inside the Ozark communities and farms, there are widows, orphans, and foreigners who need help. As a servant of Christ, I have been given many assignments, and one of these is to make sure that these widows, orphans, and outsiders have a home—to give them a place at the table. The mystery is that my joy increases as I go about the daily work that God has called me to and enabled me to do.

Oh, the unsearchable greatness of God.

***Mark Tohlen** has enjoyed a career as an aerospace engineer where he helped design and build the stealth B-2 Bomber, a flying wing. He also designed modifications to the V-22 Osprey, a plane that takes off like a helicopter. While Mark is grateful for his career, what delights him more is his family, who all love the Lord. God has blessed him with a beautiful and godly wife, two daughters, and two sons who married Christian spouses, three grandkids, with one on the way. His quiver is full. He divides his time between his home in Texas and his farm in Missouri, where he and his wife live in a 100-year-old schoolhouse, and until recently, raised Angus cows and tended a half-acre garden. Now that Mark is retired, he can risk big things for God.*

Thoughts to Ponder
from Hewn from an Ozark Rock

1. Your faith in God will influence your children.

2. Choosing to live by God's values means you will need to make difficult decisions.

3. Your joy increases as you accomplish the work God has called you to do.

How can you impact someone's faith?

Start children off on the way they should go,
and even when they are old
they will not turn from it. — Proverbs 22:6

The Ticking Alarm Clock

by Michele Stevens

An alarm is going off. *Tick-tock. Tick-tock.* Time waits for no one.

I felt time ticking away when Mom got sick. Although I grew up in church, it was the first time I truly experienced Jesus' presence and got to know Him personally. My mother felt intense pain in her stomach, and her legs swelled. She went to the hospital, but the doctors were baffled, unable to diagnose the problem. I leaned on Jesus during our time of need. I cried and prayed to Him when there were no answers. Nine months later, they finally determined that she had Crohn's disease.

Only God knows how much time we have on Earth. Mom got her affairs in order. We took her dream vacation to Maui. Less than three months later, Mom fought for her life. During her last few hours on Earth, I felt an enveloping peace. The nurses and I held hands around Mom's bed and prayed. I felt no anxiety or stress. When her spirit left her body, I was peaceful, knowing she was in a better place. It was no coincidence that she passed away on Easter, which is Resurrection Sunday. It was God's perfect plan. Her physical body was gone, but her spirit was with God in Heaven.

After Mom passed away, I struggled with grief, numbness, and pain. I buried my feelings by working, and I quit talking to God.

Time passed, but unknown to me, my life alarm clock was about to sound. Like any other morning, I woke up and climbed the stairs to awaken my daughter. I lay down with her in her bed to snuggle. Just as I touched her sheets, *Bam! Something was wrong.* The right side of my body tightened, and I couldn't move. I wanted to tell my daughter but couldn't get the words out. My daughter got up and started talking like a typical nine-year-old girl. All I could say was okay, okay, okay, over and over.

She went downstairs and said to her father, "Mom is acting weird."

I blacked out.

When I awoke, I was in my bed. My husband had helped me down the stairs to my bedroom. He thought I had finally fallen asleep, because I struggled with insomnia.

I have to get up and tell him something is wrong with my body.

I went to the kitchen and said, "I need help!" He looked at me like I was crazy.

Why can't he understand me?

I turned to walk away, and the right side of my body gave out. I collapsed on the floor. Time was ticking away. I did not realize that the short window of time to get help in this life-threatening emergency was beginning to close.

I heard my husband in the distance say, "I am calling 9-1-1 and your dad."

What? Some good-looking fireman will come in and see me half-naked, wearing only a t-shirt and panties.

My husband said I wasn't making any sense at this point, but I said, "Get my shorts!"

While my husband was pulling up my shorts, the Emergency Medical Technicians (EMTs) came in. And yes, they were good-looking. One of the EMTs asked me questions. I was unable to utter a word. For the first time, I was speechless. The EMTs hoisted me onto a stretcher, loaded me into the ambulance, gave me a shot, and immediately started oxygen.

I began to cry.

What is going on?

They took me to the local hospital. The nurse who took me for diagnostic testing told me about her husband, who experienced three strokes. The first two times, she didn't catch the warning signs. The third time, the stroke showed up on the Magnetic Resonance Imaging (MRI) machine. She felt bad. As a nurse, she thought she should have recognized the signs.

I felt Jesus say to my heart, *I was with the nurse and her husband during his strokes. I will be with you too. Trust Me, and it will be okay.*

Was it a coincidence that this nurse told me about her husband's stroke? I don't think so. God uses random events for good.

I am extremely claustrophobic, so when the nurse put me in the MRI machine, she gave me a washcloth to cover my eyes. The machine came down so close to my face. The technician told me when to hold my breath and when to release it. It was so loud. *Boom, boom, swish.* This happened repeatedly. It took about an hour for the brain scan. Normally, I would have panicked because of the closed space. I can only attribute my calmness to the power of Jesus. I had no anxiety and was completely at peace through the entire MRI.

I did not know that my family was praying. My ninety-seven-year-old grandmother asked her entire church to pray, and they asked their families to pray too. I believe in the power of prayer.

My neurologist shared the news with me that evening that I had a shower of strokes. She said I was a miracle. I believe in miracles through Jesus. He died on the cross for our sins, was resurrected again, and lives in everyone who believes in Him and repents of the wrong things they have done. Jesus shed His blood to wash away our sins.

I felt an overwhelming sense of peace the entire time I was in the hospital. I got to know Jesus on a personal level. He protected my health and revealed Himself to me through the kindness of the nurses, doctors, and staff.

By Sunday night, I was transferred to Baylor Heart Hospital in Plano, Texas. They did more tests, blood draws, shots in the stomach, and another extensive MRI. I was now a pro at covering my eyes with a washcloth so I couldn't see how near the machine was to my face. I felt Jesus was with me. I had no anxiety, stress, or worry. I put my trust in Him. I prayed to Jesus to pull me through this and to give me strength so I could continue to live and be a mom for my daughter.

My brother drove from Alabama to talk to the doctor. He had a heart arrhythmia as did my father, uncle, and two aunts. I wondered if heart arrhythmia was my problem, because it is hereditary. The doctor said it was not. I am not overweight and do not have high blood pressure or high cholesterol. So what caused the stroke?

By Tuesday night, the cardiovascular surgeon said they found what caused my stroke. Based on results from my CAT scan and EKG, they discovered a rare type of tumor on my heart called a myxoma. To my relief, he said there was nothing I did to cause this and nothing I could have done to prevent it. I needed open-heart surgery. I was still in disbelief about my stroke, and now, open-heart surgery?

I felt that Jesus was walking beside me, lifting my arms high to fight. I thought about Moses, who was instructed by God to hold his arms up during a battle. If Moses' arms were up, the Israelites continued to win. When Moses became tired and his arms dropped, the Israelites began to lose. However, Aaron and Hur came alongside Moses and held his arms up. The Israelites won that battle.

Likewise, I thought about the people who were supporting me. My grandmother and her church continued to pray for me. My friends prayed, and their church congregations prayed too. Many people were holding my arms up in prayer so I could continue doing my part of holding unwavering arms up to God. It was up to God to do the rest.

Surgery was scheduled for the morning of Friday the thirteenth. The clock had been ticking for a week after I collapsed. God was with me. I was not worried, and I attribute that to the power of prayer.

Because of the frequent vital-sign checks and tests, I didn't get much rest in the hospital. Doctors, physician assistants, nurses, and technicians seemed to be in my room around the clock. I didn't want to know any particulars of the upcoming surgery. I told myself, *I am just having routine surgery.* I didn't give it a name. The atmosphere in my hospital room was positive and uplifting as my sister made sure no one negative was around.

When I was going through the stroke and heart surgery, Jesus was with me every step of the way. The stroke saved my life, because if the stroke had not occurred, my heart condition would never have been discovered. Again, there are no coincidences with God. His timing is perfect. I had complete peace—no stress or anxiety. I trusted Jesus completely. He protected me during and after the stroke and during the open-heart surgery. I put my life completely in His hands.

The day after my surgery, one of my best friends, Paula, died of a heart attack. She was the same age as me. We do not know when our time on Earth will be over. It is all in God's perfect timing. I believe she is at peace with Jesus in Heaven, where there is no pain, crying, or suffering.

Since I have gone through this life-changing event, I do not take a single day for granted. I know how precious life is. Jesus Christ changed me. I recognize the beauty of God's creation when I see the sunset or hear my daughter laugh. Jesus is omniscient and omnipresent. He holds time in His hands.

Michele Stevens is a wife, mother, and comes from a family of five. Through many life challenges and health issues, she has victoriously come through each of them with the peace of Christ. She currently attends Watermark Community Church and is a Realtor.

Thoughts to Ponder
from The Ticking Alarm Clock

1. There are no coincidences with God.

2. God can keep the storm from blowing away your peace.

3. No one is promised tomorrow.

What makes your life valuable?

All the days ordained for me were written in your book before one of them came to be. — Psalm 139:16

Seeds of Faith

by Mark Dann

I was raised in a conservative Jewish household. My father was the only one of four siblings who followed Judaism. His father was Jewish, but his mother was of the Christian faith. My mother's side of the family consisted of conservative and orthodox Jews. At the age of thirteen, I prepared for my Bar Mitzvah. I could not fully grasp how to read Hebrew from the Torah, so I memorized my entire Torah portion. The Rabbi agreed to record it on a cassette tape. This is the way I was able to "read" my Torah portion out loud.

My wife was raised in the Christian faith. She was active in Bible study groups, and I was proud and respected her for that. When we married, we chose to have an off-site Jewish wedding. Before having kids, we decided we would introduce our children to both religious backgrounds so they would have an understanding and respect for both. However, we agreed that they would eventually follow the Christian faith through our leadership and direction.

I grew up with friends from faith-based families. I met Jim in college. We became best friends and eventually participated in each other's weddings. Jim took me to church with him, and when we attended church or discussed religion, he wanted me to be engaged in the conversation. Jim was respectful of who I was and my religious upbringing. I think he really wanted to convert me but never really said that to me.

Years later after we graduated and were deep into our careers and raising families, we remained connected by phone, weekend visits, and special occasions. We were open with each other and talked about anything that came to our minds.

In November 2006, we met at Texas A&M before a football game. Jim did not go into the stadium for the game, because he needed to take his father home, and he had his two daughters with him. Jim and I hugged and said our goodbyes. We tightly embraced each other as we stood in the middle of the crowd. This was not uncommon, but it felt different.

I soon found out why. That was the last time I ever talked to

Jim. He died of a brain aneurysm while driving his father and two daughters home. I got the phone call halfway through the fourth quarter. I rushed to the hospital to be by his side as he breathed his last breath and entered Heaven. I am convinced that God wanted us to see each other that day. Jim left behind his wonderful wife and six children.

Jim was the type of person who made friends with everyone. He had a wonderful personality and a way of touching people's lives through his faith and acts of kindness. When he went through difficult times, he never wavered in his faith nor in his love toward family and friends.

At his funeral, the church had standing room only, with people of all ages. On that day, I found new seeds of faith and a deeper meaning of God.

Several years later, I visited Jim's gravesite and dropped a small written note into a crack in the dirt, which disappeared into the ground when I let go of it. On the note I said, "I will be back to see you, and I will never forget you."

In the last few years, I have engaged in contemporary Christian music. I have over one hundred songs on my iPhone and listen to them as I walk, ride my bike, or exercise. For me, the songs' music, words, and messages are inspirational, spiritual, and powerful. Recently, while lying in bed one night, I thought, *Why am I so drawn to this type of music? I know I like all kinds of music, including Country, Oldies, and Top 40, but Christian music? Could it be that God is trying to tell me something by planting more seeds? Or could it be that Jim, looking down from Heaven, is trying to deepen my faith? Or could it be that I was just in search of more faith in my life?* I continued to think about it for months as I listened to and focused more on the meaning and messages of what I felt was God's own music.

On September 24th, 2016, I went to Boerne, Texas, for one of Jim's daughter's weddings. Before the wedding, I returned to visit Jim's gravesite as I had promised. It was a nice sunny day. I knelt on Jim's grave in front of his beautiful headstone, and I prayed out loud to God.

"I believe in Jesus Christ, and I accept Him as my Lord and Savior. I want your Son, Jesus Christ, to accept me and forgive me for all my past sins."

I spent the next hour walking through the cemetery, still praying out loud and soul searching. Finally, this was the day I decided I wanted Jesus Christ.

As I walked out of the cemetery, I felt different. I felt fresh, cleansed, pure, calm, and at peace. I knew that I had just become part of a new family and a newly found faith.

In 2016, I received a Christmas card from my brother-in-law with a flier inside, which he thought might interest me. It was an invitation to Beth Sar Shalom Congregational Church, also known as Sojourner Ministries.

The flier said, "Jewish Believers" and "Exploring the Jewish Heart of Christianity." I didn't understand it and threw it away. For the next several days I thought about that flier and what it said across the top. *Who am I? What am I? What do I believe in? Well, I am a Jew. I am proud of my heritage and upbringing. Just a few months ago, I gave my life to Jesus Christ the Son of God.* I had asked for His forgiveness of my sins and for Him to be my Lord and Savior. Then it hit me. *That's it, that's me. That's who I am. In my heart, I am a Jewish believer.*

I ran to the trash and found the flier I had thrown away. I looked up this Messianic congregation and liked what I saw. It would be unique to have the perspective of both Judaism and Christianity together in the same sermon.

During this time, I received a flier from Lake Pointe Church, a contemporary Christian church that was opening in the neighborhood. After attending both churches and their Bible studies, I joined both.

I plan to attend both churches as much as I can, as a stepping stone in furthering my journey and search of faith through prayer, education, and serving others.

Back when my journey started and seeds were just being planted, I felt more self-centered, purposeless, and going my own way. Now, I feel much more Christ-centered, purposeful, and directed in God's way.

For most of my professional life, I was busy in my career and focused on making money. I wasn't spending everything we made on a lavish lifestyle, but we had nice things and a nice lifestyle. I'm not making excuses, but I'm merely illustrating how we tend to get so wrapped up in our own lives that we sometimes forget the "big picture."

I had almost everything anyone would want—a great job, great wife, great family, great home. I was content and happy, but I didn't feel fulfilled. I asked, S*o is this it?* As the seeds of faith were being planted, I began searching for faith and more in life.

I believe Jim planted seeds in my journey of faith. My wife set the example of perseverance, and my brother-in-law gave me the extra push I needed. Most of all, I believe it was God, through a culmination of many events in my life, Who brought me to faith. I am forever grateful that I chose to accept Jesus Christ.

My journey of faith will continue through God's music and by attending church and study groups. I am reading the Bible for the first time so I can learn God's Word. My plan of serving others will be through the Children's Advocacy Center, mission trips, and maybe even a trip to Israel.

It's taken all my life to get to this point. Time to get to work.

Mark Dann *resides in Dallas, Texas, and is blessed with a wonderful wife and two grown boys. It has been over four years since he accepted Christ as his Lord and Savior. He can say with certainty that his life has changed in many wonderful ways, both internally and externally. He's come to realize that one's "testimony" and "journey" never really end. To do good works, to study God's Word, and to be as Christ-like as we humanly can be, all these things will continue until we reach eternal life in Heaven. Contact Mark at* **MarkWDann@gmail.com.**

Thoughts to Ponder
from Seeds of Faith

1. You plant seeds of faith in people's lives by respectfully sharing Jesus with them.

2. God uses different people and situations to draw you to Him.

3. There is more to life than worldly success.

> ## *Who planted seeds of faith in your life?*

I planted the seed, Apollos watered it, but God has been making it grow. — 1 Corinthians 3:6

No One Believed Me
by Kim Lakin Creger

I was confused and terrified. *Should I freeze, fight, or escape in flight?* I chose to run out of the basement as fast as I could. At too young an age, this was my first introduction to sexual abuse. No one had warned me.

Only five years earlier, I was born in Rapid City, South Dakota. My mom was sixteen years old and still going to high school when I was delivered. She was a spitfire. Being such a young mom, having two children under the age of three, and going through a divorce by the age of twenty-one was evidence of her independence.

Looking back, I believe my mom acted like a typical twenty-something-year-old. Because of her two children, she didn't have the freedom she desired. After she met my stepdad, I was responsible for my brother and had duties like changing his diaper.

With Mom married to my stepdad, outsiders thought I lived in a stable home. She was a paralegal for a local judge, and my stepdad was an animal control officer. On their weekends and days off, drugs were the priority, not the children. She shared too much information about her life while I was still young. Sometimes I was treated as a child or teen, and sometimes I had the responsibilities of an adult. Most of the time, their expectations were just whatever was convenient for them. I was confused. I felt like I was never good enough.

From age five until seventeen, I was sexually abused by people both in and out of the family. When I was five, two teenage brothers, cousins of my friend, walked around their house with their pants unzipped. Also, my parents were open and sometimes walked around with barely anything on. This caused me to question what was normal.

One time, while I visited my friend's house, the brothers separated my friend and me, and one of them trapped me in a closet. He was aggressive in wanting me to touch him in inappropriate ways. That was when I ran from the basement as fast as I could. On my way out, I saw my friend being abused. In my five-year-old mind, I thought she must have been more mature than me to be doing that. From then on, I avoided going into my friend's house. What I know now is they were all being abused.

My life brightened at age six. My grandmother found a church that would take my aunt, who was two years older, and me to Sunday school. I loved getting dressed up for church but mostly loved learning about Jesus. I always felt very safe and happy when I was at church. I think, even though my mom didn't go with us, she knew from her Baptist upbringing that it was important for us to have a spiritual foundation. As my brother got older, he went with us. However, he was a handful and ran up and down the halls. Our parents thought it was a great way to sleep in.

I believe God knew how desperately I needed Him. Having that foundation is what helped me forgive and heal.

Shortly after starting Sunday school, I became extremely sick. It took a couple of months to figure out what was wrong with me. My doctor said there must be something going on, something I was hiding, or something was happening at school that made me not want to attend. Both of those things were correct.

Something else bad happened in my body that almost killed me. When the doctors finally figured it out, my appendix ruptured. I was a sick little girl for nine months. I was in and out of the hospital and had two operations. I missed most of my second-grade year. This led to being held back in the third grade, which was another traumatic event for me.

One day while I was watching TV and recovering from my appendectomy, there was a knock on the door. My stepdad opened the door and told visitors from the church that he didn't want them to come in. I was upset that I couldn't pray with them. I'm sure my parents didn't want them in to see all their drug paraphernalia that was lying around the house. When I was well, I was the one to hide the "stuff" when people came over.

Shortly after my recovery, we moved a few blocks away from the teenagers who abused my friend and me. I felt safer. I no longer went to my friend's house to play, but she came to mine. I learned later that the brothers were only three and six years older than my friend and me. Because they were so aggressive, I thought they were a lot older.

Between the ages of eight and twelve, I was frequently cornered by male cousins in my family. When we played hide and seek in the dark, I was often found and "felt up." At the time, I did not know this behavior was wrong. *Didn't all guys do this? Isn't that what girls are for?*

At age twelve, my stepdad sexually abused me six times. He finally stopped when I sobbed and told him I did not like it. However, the damage was already done. Terrible thoughts of what he said he was going to do haunted me. To make matters worse, this was the time our stepdad was trying to adopt us. Later he told me that he stopped because I pointed to the judge and said, "I want *you* to be my dad." When the judge asked if I wanted to be adopted by my stepdad, I said, "I don't think I have a choice."

By thirteen, I was interested in boys and ready to be free from the sexual, mental, and physical abuse that haunted me in my home. The drugs in our house were shared with the children, along with weird religions and Yahtzee parties that involved drugs. I've always thought of my childhood as living in a "free love" atmosphere. Great for pedophiles and druggies— not so much for children.

We moved to Washington state to open a family restaurant when I was fourteen. There I met my first real boyfriend and fell madly in love. All I wanted was to escape. One night, my parents caught me trying to sneak out to meet him. My stepdad threw me through a wall, and I decided it was finally time to tell my mom that he had molested me. She dismissed it and told me she was abused as a child as well. We did go to one family counseling session where we were told we had a nice family.

I spiraled downward and became rebellious. I ran away with my boyfriend to Florida for three months.

When I got pregnant with my daughter at age eighteen, I realized that my life needed to change. I wasn't going to let my baby girl fall into the same abusive lifestyle that I had gone through. At nineteen, I became a single mom. I met my husband while I was pregnant. That's another story. I wanted to do all that I could to break the abuse cycle and make sure my baby grew up healthy, happy, and free from knowing anything about abuse. I didn't know how, but I did know how *not* to raise children.

When my children were growing up, I didn't have enough information and tools about child sexual abuse prevention. Now I have body safety books on my grandchildren's bookshelf to empower them to know they are the boss of their bodies. All I knew to do with my children was to be where they were to keep them safe. God impressed upon my heart Isaiah 40:31: "But those who hope in the Lord will renew their strength. They will soar on wings like eagles; they will run and not grow weary, they will walk and not be faint." I believe God raised me on wings like eagles and strengthened me to change my family's history and proactively protect my children.

For the past thirty-two years, I've been a mom to three healthy and wonderful, now-grown kids. I have two son-in-loves and am Grandma to five awesome grandkids. My abuse was not something I shared with my children as they were growing up, since it wasn't their burden to carry. However, I now share as much as they want to know, which has been different for each of my grown children. I did ask them all to take a two-hour class so we are all on the same page with safety for their children.

I've learned over the years that God's love is unconditional, and I am worthy. The unconditional love my children and grandchildren have given me is such a blessing. While I still have many unanswered questions, I have seen God use horrible events to bring good. Proverbs 3:5–6 says, "Trust in the Lord with all your heart and lean not on your own understanding; in all your ways submit to Him, and He will make your paths straight."

I've spent many years in different kinds of therapy and counseling. After years of healing in my inner child, I find I've deepened my healing by using my experiences to help others. I know my true healing and forgiveness have come from God.

I became an advocate for children twenty-five years ago, volunteering and working in public schools, children's ministries, and other church affiliations. My children's advocacy and volunteer work were birthed from a need to be there for my children and keep them safe. My heart has desired to teach

144

children about Jesus, how much He loves them, and how He will always be there for them when others let them down.

Unfortunately, I've encountered many abused children in my work and volunteer careers. Because of my experiences, I have always given children hope, grace, forgiveness, and unconditional love that they don't always get at home. Even if they never remember my name, I want them to feel loved and to grow in their love for Jesus.

While attending a Women of Faith conference eighteen years ago, God revealed to me that I should speak to educate others about child sexual abuse prevention. That revelation was scary. God spent years preparing my heart and equipping me to speak to large crowds. I have only spoken about my abuse openly in the last four years.

I became an Authorized Facilitator and then a Certified Instructor for the Stewards of Children program at the Darkness to Light (D2L) organization. The program's focus is on child sexual abuse prevention using a five-step method that incorporates true stories from survivors.

My research says that one in ten children will be abused before their eighteenth birthday. I love that I can educate and empower other adults to help prevent abuse. This takes the burden from children so they understand what is happening or know that others are believing what they say.

My target audience is churches. Unfortunately, churches are one of the places child abusers hideout. An abuser could be the person sitting next to you in church or someone working in the youth group. My goal is to get into churches before something happens. The church needs to be the voice for those who need help voicing the truth. Believing the child is the first step to any healing.

Last year I also became an Authorized Facilitator for the Monique Burr Foundation for Children (MBF). I am passionate about training children to protect themselves from bullying, cyberbullying, child abuse, bodily harm, digital abuse, and other digital dangers by using the MBF Safety Matters Safety Rules. The MBF has joined with D2L to make it simple for adults and children to learn easy steps to stay safe and keep others safe.

I prayed for my parents to know Christ as their Lord and

Savior. That prayer was answered for my mom six months before she went home to be with Jesus. This happened after she started working for the church that she attended. She was fifty-four years old when God took her to Heaven.

Five years after my mom passed away, my stepdad showed up one Sunday at the church I attended. He was baptized six months later. I attended his new Christian class with him. Because he is still alive and was one of my abusers, I sometimes feel odd openly discussing my childhood abuse and training on abuse prevention. However, he knows where my family and I stand. Today he lives close by and is one of my biggest advocates for the work I do.

When I was abused, I learned to rely on God when no one believed me. I am amazed at the path God has taken me through so I can now help others. Currently, I have trained over six hundred adults in the Stewards of Children program, and I know that I am just starting my journey. I'm ready and open to what God has planned for me next.

"For I know the plans I have for you," declares the Lord,
"plans to prosper you and not to harm you,
plans to give you hope and a future."
Jeremiah 29:11

Kim Lakin Creger *was six years old when she was sent to Sunday school on a bus. She believes God knew how desperately she needed Jesus as a foundation, especially at the time of abuse in her young life. As an adult, Kim's mission is to educate adults and children about body safety and child sexual abuse prevention by providing Darkness to Light, Stewards of Children, and The Monique Burr classes. Contact Kim at* **KimLakinCreger.com, Kim Creger** *on* **LinkedIn,** *or* **Facebook.com/SoarOnEaglesWings16.**

Thoughts to Ponder

from No One Believed Me

1. You need to be aware of child sexual abuse prevention.

2. True healing and forgiveness come only from God.

3. God uses your experiences to bring healing to others.

How can your healing help others?

You intended to harm me, but God intended it for good to accomplish what is now being done, the saving of many lives. — Genesis 50:20

My Thorn in the Flesh
by William Comer

When we come down with any illness, one of our first thoughts is a countdown to when we will be over it. After twenty-eight years of perfect health, in the spring of 1976, I started feeling bad at a time I could not afford to be ill. I had finished four years in the Navy, gone back to college for a semester, graduated in Chemical Engineering, and started a new career. Forty-four years later, I am still counting down the day I will be over it.

After a full year of going from doctor to doctor and weighing less than 100 pounds, I went to the Kelsey-Sebold Clinic in Houston, Texas, and was diagnosed with Crohn's disease, which has no known cause or cure. It is interesting how our focus changes when we hear bad news. The Lord had my attention.

After dealing with Crohn's for many years and realizing that it was not going away, I believed I would never live to see my children grow up, keep a job until retirement, retire, or see my grandchildren. This belief was reinforced when we first moved to Baton Rouge in 1989. I met a neighbor and also a church member who had Crohn's. They were both disabled and died during the next five years.

About the time I believed I was going to survive Crohn's, I came down with melanoma cancer in 2001 and was given a one-in-three chance of survival. In 2009, about the time I believed I would survive the most dangerous form of skin cancer, I came down with colon cancer, which is common for individuals with Crohn's. Well, by the grace of God, I kept my job, lived to see our three fine sons grow up, retired at sixty-five in 2013, and at seventy-two have better health than I did at fifty. I now have three grandsons, Greyson, Alexander, and Ethan.

Now that you know the story, as Paul Harvey used to say, "What is the rest of the story?"

One lesson I learned is that most of the best long-term events in my life started with an event that I would not have chosen and was very difficult. After high school, I wanted to study engineering but had not properly prepared for college. My mom was a camp nurse during the summers. The camp director wrote a recommendation for me to attend Marion Military Institute in 1966–1967, where I could take both college and high school courses to make up for what I did not do in high school. It was difficult, but I excelled academically for the first time, while also preparing for college. I entered the college of Chemical Engineering at the University of Alabama in the fall of 1967.

In January of 1971, I drew a draft lottery number of 64, and they were drafting through 119. So I joined the Navy for four years. I enjoyed my time in the Navy and met my wife. I developed financial habits of avoiding credit and debt, which was a benefit to me throughout my life, and I learned skills that were as valuable to me as my engineering degree.

Early in my struggle, I realized that I was not guaranteed a single day on this earth and that God has numbered my days before the foundations of the earth were laid down. This was a turning point for me in dealing with Crohn's disease. Even if I had perfect health, I was not guaranteed another day. This was the changing of head knowledge into heart knowledge.

Several times when I felt down, and yes, even sorry for myself, I weighed the issue against what it could be or what others were dealing with. I could only be thankful and less complaining.

Helen Keller said it very well. "I cried because I had no shoes until I met a man who had no feet."

Five years into dealing with Crohn's, I made an appointment with my doctor to express my frustration and tell him something had to change. My doctor was on vacation and his backfill came in and said, "Do you realize what a devastating and disabling disease Crohn's is and what a light case you have?" He explained what many of his patients were dealing with, and I realized that my case was difficult but not devastating, disabling, or as bad as a vast majority of others.

Something changed that day. My attitude changed from a focus on what I did not like about the circumstance to thanking God for the many blessings I had been given. I have a good job, an exceptional wife who never complained about the situation, wonderful parents, two good brothers, three fine children, and the Lord and Creator of the universe by my side. All I had done was complain about my physical ailment that, compared to many others, was manageable. It is amazing how we lose perspective at times.

I also realized how blessed I was to complete my tour in the Navy, graduate from college, marry my lovely wife of forty-seven years, and have our first son, David, who was conceived before the onset of Crohn's. I doubt that any of these events could have happened if I had Crohn's.

We often reflect on what a blessing and joy our first son, David, was and how we thought he was going to be a burden that we could not handle when I was so sick and was still undiagnosed. I am thankful that the only option we had was to trust in the Lord and not turn to the solution that our secular society offers. I was also fortunate enough to respond well to treatment so I could remain employed. We were then blessed with two more children, Alan and Sean.

I know the Bible says no one is righteous and Job's suffering was not a punishment from God. Why was this happening to me? While I asked myself what I had done to deserve this, I realized that the last thing I wanted from God was what I deserved.

The salvation and forgiveness I experience from faith in Christ are not of my merit, but a gift from God. We experience love and faith in Christ only because He first loved us, and the Father draws us toward Him. If we put our faith in Christ and Him alone, then we become children of God. The Father disciplines the children He loves with the purpose of making us more like His Son, our Lord and Savior Jesus Christ. The Bible tells us that even Jesus in His human form learned obedience through that which He suffered.

I had wanted to have it my way and the easy way. As the years and decades passed, I could only complain less and give thanks to God more. It is my sincere desire that this testimony will help you to trust God on the front end of any challenge you may encounter and that you will know His heart of faithfulness.

- "And we know that in all things God works for the good of those who love him, who have been called according to his purpose. For those God foreknew he also predestined to be conformed to the image of his Son, that he might be the firstborn among many brothers and sisters." — Romans 8:28–29

- "Son though he was, he learned obedience from what he suffered." — Hebrew 5:8
- "There is no one righteous, not even one." — Romans 3:10
- "For it is by grace you have been saved, through faith—and this is not from yourselves, it is the gift of God." — Ephesians 2:8
- "No one can come to me unless the Father who sent me draws them, and I will raise them up at the last day." — John 6:44
- "We love because he first loved us." — 1 John 4:19
- "Very truly I tell you, whoever hears my word and believes him who sent me has eternal life and will not be judged but has crossed over from death to life." — John 5:24

William Comer graduated from Childersburg, Alabama high school in 1966. He attended Marion Military Institute and graduated from the University of Alabama with a Bachelor of Science in Chemical Engineering. William was a United States Navy Tradevman at Pinecastle Electronic Warfare Range in Astor Park, Florida. He married Marilly Watkins in 1973 and has three sons, David, Alan, and Sean. William has been employed by PPG Industries, Ashland Oil, and Exxon Mobil, and retired in 2013. His hobbies include electronics, hiking, guitar, banjo, and mandolin. Contact William at WAComer@aol.com or 225-202-2953.

Thoughts to Ponder
from My Thorn in the Flesh

1. Count your blessings, not your problems.

2. Difficult events can produce long-term benefits.

3. Be grateful for each day.

> ### *How many blessings can you name?*

Praise be to the God and Father of our Lord Jesus Christ, Who has blessed us in the heavenly realms with every spiritual blessing in Christ. — Ephesians 1:3

The Lake and the Holy Spirit
by Sue Z. McGray

The lake, the lake, the lake. I heard these words as if they were shouted from a rooftop. The Holy Spirit gave me these two words, and they changed the direction of my life.

I married too young. I graduated from high school on a Tuesday and was married the following Saturday. I was not ready for marriage, but I did so because of pressure from him. I felt I had no choice. I wanted to believe he loved me, even with his control and manipulation issues. Unfortunately, I knew nothing about the signs of an abuser.

I became codependent, not from chemical dependency but from an unhealthy lifestyle. I possessed no decision-making capabilities. Because of low self-esteem, I questioned any thought or idea that I had. I was concerned only with other people's reality, not my own.

After years of being put down and told that no one else would ever want me, my self-worth was at rock-bottom. The only way I could function was to act as if I knew absolutely nothing. The verbal abuse had always been there, but I made excuses for him. When my mom made comments about the way he talked to me, I defended him, saying, "He doesn't mean what he says. That is just the way he is."

As time went on, the emotional and verbal abuse became worse. Even though I was told that physical abuse would follow, by the time it started, I thought I deserved it. *If I had not made him mad or if I had not said or done something, he would not have lost his temper.* Yes, it must have been my fault, and he made sure that I knew it was my fault.

His abuse was followed by affairs. I knew about the affairs but did not confront him. I became an emotionally sick person. It is amazing what a wife will put up with when she chooses to live in denial.

My life became more and more stressful, and I was learning about codependency. A friend gave me a book called *Codependency No More* by Melody Beattie. This book changed my life. I realized for the first time that I had an illness called codependency. It was like going to the doctor and getting a name for my symptoms. It did not change anything, but I realized that I was not alone and could get help. I then joined a codependency group.

My parents lived ninety minutes away. When I went to visit, I felt impressed to stop by a drug store owned by my friend Patty and her husband. She invited me to her stockroom to visit. I sat on a box.

Patty looked at me and said, "Sue, what is it going to take?" She did not know my circumstances, but she sensed that I was not only in crisis but needed to get my life right with God.

The following week, I surrendered my life to Christ. I am so thankful to Patty for being there for me. Many mornings, she called and said that she had been awakened during the night to pray for me.

One morning while eating breakfast, my husband said, "I ought to just kill you."

Because of what I learned in the codependency group, I said, "That is not acceptable." I stood and went to the kitchen. I knew I was in trouble when I walked out.

Again, he said, "I ought to just kill you."

I said, "That is not acceptable." I ran out the door, got into my car, and pulled out of the driveway. I was shaking. In my rear-view mirror, I saw that he was following me.

The night before, I had visualized which way I should go if I had to get away quickly. I went the way that I had seen in my semi-sleep state. Only a couple of blocks away, I was stopped by a red light. I saw a policeman, and I started blowing my car horn repeatedly. When I blew my horn, several policemen gathered around me, as if they had been waiting for me.

My plans that day were to pick up a business associate and drive to Atlanta for a meeting. So I convinced the police that I would go on my business trip and everything would be fine when I returned.

One officer wasn't convinced. She knelt beside my car door, got in my face, and pointed her finger at me. "Let me tell you how it is. If you do not go downtown right now and get an order of protection, it will be too late when you return from your business trip."

I was filled with fear, and I did what she told me to do. I knew it would make my husband angry, and he would make my life even more miserable. I took my business associate with me, got an order of protection, and left town for our trip.

When I returned, I did not go home. The anxiety was unbearable. In thirty years, I had never gone anywhere without my husband's knowledge. My nerves were on edge, and my emotions were going crazy. *What would I do?* I had nowhere to go.

I heard there were shelters for abused women, so I called the local shelter and they had no available beds. The lady at the shelter was extremely kind and asked if I had access to money or credit cards so I could get a hotel room. Fortunately, I had a credit card in my name, which my husband did not know about.

Without knowing what I was going to do, I headed to a nearby town and found a hotel. At first, I could not make myself go inside. I circled the hotel several times, crying my heart out, feeling desperate and alone. Finally, I went into the hotel and registered for a room.

The next day, I attended a church in the area. I have no idea what the sermon was about, but after the service, a couple introduced themselves to me, realized that I was in trouble, and took me to their home. They lived in a three-bedroom apartment with their two teenage daughters. They gave me one of the girls' bedrooms. This was a time of refreshment and rest for me. After living with the couple and their teenage daughters a couple of months, I decided it was time to move on.

My daughter was attending college and shared a house with a friend. I thought going to her house would be a good idea, so I spent the night. The next day I looked for a place of my own. Living out of my car was not an option. I still believed my marriage could be fixed.

At that time, I was very fragile. For many, it takes several severe abuses before a spouse will leave. I had left once before. My daughter and her friends moved me the first time. I hired a young couple to help me move my things back to the house. My husband and I never discussed why I left. I did not want that to happen again.

I never thought that I would have to move out again.

However, I was learning more about domestic violence and codependency. Because I did not want the children to come from a broken home, I stayed in the situation. Eventually, I realized that I was teaching them that it was okay to be treated that way and that it was okay to treat their spouses that way. I had to get well for me and them. I had to find the courage to focus on me first.

I found a one-bedroom apartment and paid the deposit plus one month's rent. My only possessions were a Papasan chair and a few clothes. The apartment was furnished with a stove and refrigerator. I bought a sofa and used it for my bed. For Mother's Day, my birthday, and Christmas, my kids bought me a washer, dryer, TV, and other household items.

Life was simple, uncluttered, and blissfully uneventful. Other than my children, few were invited to my "sweet place." As I continued to seek Christian counseling, I finally began to heal. But I still was not ready to give up on my marriage.

One Monday morning, I agreed to have an early lunch with my estranged husband. I refused to believe I could not keep our marriage together. Because I had been raised to believe divorce was not acceptable, I could not bear the guilt of hurting my parents.

Once inside the restaurant, I went to the salad bar. As I reached for the lettuce, I heard the words, *the lake, the lake, the lake*. I didn't know what to make of it. The lake had not been part of our lives for many years.

As I sat down at our table, I said, "Did you go to the lake over the weekend"?

He was stunned, agitated, and nervous. "I knew you had someone watching me. Let's get out of here now."

Our lunch ended before I had even taken a bite. He stormed off to pay the bill, and I followed him to his truck. I had struck a nerve and was unaware of what would happen next. I didn't know anything about "the lake," but I felt God was up to something.

Once we were in his vehicle, I sensed his anger.

He said, "I knew you had a private investigator following me."

What? I had not even thought of that. I said nothing. I did

156

not want him to know that I didn't know anything about the lake.

He dropped me off at my office and left.

I soon got calls from both children saying he had called, explaining that he was only at the lake to call off his affair.

Wow! This was information I did not know how to handle. I thought we were working on our marriage, but his agenda was something else. I didn't feel that I should tell the kids or anyone else about what God had revealed to me. I knew God loved me, but to love me this much was overwhelming. Sometimes, God does things that are just too big to explain. For years, I did not tell my kids or anyone else about the lake story.

A few days later, I asked my parents to meet me for lunch. I sat across from my dad and said, "I must tell you something."

My dad said, "Honey, I know."

"But how do you know? Who told you? How could you know?"

My dad said, "Honey, God told me."

Wow! I never knew what God told my dad, but from that day forward, my parents were supportive in every way. It is hard to explain, but as painful as it was to experience the separation and divorce, I had total peace. When I laid my head down at night, I felt engulfed in a soft cloud with protection all around me.

One day as I was leaving my parents' house, my dad said, "Honey, I am praying for God to send a godly man to you."

I was not happy with him asking God to send me a husband. I said, "I am doing just fine, and I don't need a man to take care of me."

Even though I went through a lot of pain, I experienced much growth. I learned to hear God's voice and trust my decisions. I was content living alone, and I believed without a doubt that I would never remarry.

I lived in a one-bedroom apartment for four years. It was a peaceful time for me. The first year, I slept a lot and felt my body and mind healing. I spent the next three years building my business. I didn't date and was never lonely.

I desired to build a home where I could easily host friends and family. So I started a dream book. I cut out magazine pictures of things I wanted for my dream house. I took my dream book everywhere. I went to see a home builder and then a banker. I knew nothing about building a house, but I learned to take one step at a time. This was a time for growing again. To complete and furnish my home, I used my dream book. About eighteen months later, I moved into my house.

At about the same time, God brought a godly man into my life. Duane and his beautiful red-headed daughter moved to Nashville, and a friend introduced us.

Duane and I got married, and we still live in my dream house. Our three children are now grown, with children of their own.

Life is good. The friend who introduced Duane and me said, "Don't let what you've lived be wasted." With Duane's encouragement, I wrote a book, *Becoming Visible: Letting Go of the Things that Hide Your True Beauty*. My parents are gone now, but I like to think that I honor them by living my life the way they taught me.

Sue Z. McGray is an author and speaker. She serves on the board with Morning Star Sanctuary, a Christian safe place for women and children. She also serves on the Advisory Board for Christian Women in Media. Sue's hobby is oil painting. She and her husband, Duane, have three adult children and five granddaughters. They live in Nashville, Tennessee. In her book, Becoming Visible: Letting Go of the Things that Hide Your True Beauty, *Sue shares how readers can let go of the things that hide their God-given beauty and how to trust God for their peace. Contact Sue at* **SueZ@SueZMcGray.com** *or find her website at* **https://www.SueZMcGray.com.**

Thoughts to Ponder
from The Lake and the Holy Spirit

1. The Holy Spirit reveals what you cannot know on your own.

2. God has a reliable compass for your life.

3. God has all the love you can contain.

When has God given you peace in the midst of turmoil?

---

*When He, the Spirit of truth, comes,
He will guide you into all the truth. — John 16:13*

Never Give Up
by Cathy Kilpatrick

Martin Luther King once said, "We must accept finite disappointment, but never lose infinite hope." This quote summarizes the journey we endured after the birth of our son, Will. Our baby boy was born two months early, and we were scared to death after a spontaneous birth. As soon as Will emerged, he was whisked away to the Neo-Natal Intensive Care Unit (NICU), a place for seriously ill baby patients. I wasn't even able to hold him. Often, when a baby enters NICU, there is a chance the baby may never go home. We knew that was a possibility for us.

Not knowing what the future held, at the two-month mark of our baby's hospital stay, we dedicated and baptized little Will to the Lord in the NICU. We dressed up for this special occasion, brought in our church deacon, and asked the Lord to bless this little guy who had so much difficulty being born and living life.

That was the first time hospital personnel let me hold him for more than a few minutes. Will was hooked up to life support, tubes, oxygen, a g-tube, and chylothorax drainage tubes. Because of the restraints, holding him was quite difficult. We had a big half-sheet cake to celebrate with the NICU staff. We sang, prayed, and dedicated him to God. Inside the NICU, we were placed in an isolation room because of Will's infection with Methicillin-Resistant Staphylococcus Aureus (MRSA), a bacterium that causes infections in different parts of the body. The medical staff did not want him contaminating other patients.

We were at the hospital day after day, week after week, and month after month for half a year. One thing after another. Complication after complication. Everything that could have gone wrong went wrong. The loss of function equaled more equipment. But little Will kept hanging on, and we kept being hopeful that he would come home. We called him God's Will, because he kept surviving. The blood clot in the superior vena cava that became infected with MRSA turned into sepsis, which meant his whole body was infected. It was deadly, yet he lived.

Many days it was "touch and go."

When we baptized Will in that private isolation room, we didn't know that there was a huge crowd gathered outside the room. It was a group of staff members from the entire hospital. The chaplains, the president and CEO of the hospital, surgeons, nurses, doctors, therapists, students, and volunteers. Everyone from suits to scrubs, lab coats, techs, and aides came to worship with us. These were not curious onlookers. They came in solidarity, in hope for us and with us. We had no idea anyone was even there until the ceremony was over. That's when we turned around to find that the entire NICU was packed with worshipers. What a gift to know we were not alone. They came voluntarily, seeking the Lord.

How can you not believe in God?

They didn't come for the donuts and coffee. They came for worship. Funny, we always thought we were alone in that isolation room, but we weren't. The glass walls were situated so others could see us. More than anything, we knew God was with us in that room, day after day.

When we baptized and dedicated Will to the Lord on July 25, 1996, we placed a stake in the ground. For what God had planned, we had faith that God would get the credit, but we surely didn't want Will to die. He couldn't help being born too early. Sometimes we felt like this was all about God doing the impossible through Will. The medical team had a list of all the things that were wrong with him, but we knew God was the authority, not a list of medical problems. We said, "Let's wait and see. Perhaps the Lord is in this place." Because of his damaged lungs and reduced lung capacity, the head surgeon said, "Will will never be an Olympic athlete." I thought, *Well, perhaps he can be a surgeon.*

We didn't give up. Events in the NICU were overwhelming— very overwhelming. We became discouraged as even more complications developed from the original complications. We weren't always good sports about this series of circumstances, but we were hopeful and hanging on. I believe prayer saved Will's life, and because of our faith, God gave us more time with little Will.

There were warnings before Will's birth. Early on in my

pregnancy, my doctor said something was wrong and we needed to do some testing. My husband, Micky, said, "No more testing. We *are not* going to do anything differently." Micky could see where "this testing" was going, but I did not. I wonder how many women have been misguided to abort, because there was a "problem" or an "issue" with the pregnancy. I think it was at this point that we were just going to take whatever God was going to give us. We trusted Him, not the world. I credit my husband for faith and patience in this process.

Will went on to have issues throughout his short life, but he did live to be six years old. God was gracious, because at the time Will passed away, he was not on any form of life support. We always thought we would have to make some serious decisions. However, we did not have to "pull the plug" during numerous situations in the NICU. We watched other parents appeal to the hospital ethics committee to discontinue heroic measures. Will's heart simply stopped one day. It was a shock, because he had survived so many complications and had defied all the odds. But God's timing was perfect, not the timing that statistics decided.

After the autopsy, we had a conference with Will's medical team, and the very first thing they said was, "We don't know how this child lived or lived so long. And we don't know how he died, other than his heart stopped. We don't know how he could have lived with a compromised immune system, organ atrophy, diminished lung capacity, and rheumatoid arthritis that paralyzed internal organs, and we don't know how he died." The medical team said this child lived because of the care he got at home. I believe that was code for the fact that he received prayers and love. I think it was also a code for, *How can you not believe in God?* I'm so grateful that God spared us so much heartache even though there was tremendous grief. God is our authority, not the world.

We never lost hope for Will's recovery. After he defied all odds, we thought he would be a survivor and eventually grow up to be strong, but it was not God's plan.

God is our authority, not the world. We would never trade the six years we had with Will. We chose what was everlasting, not what was easy. We chose no more testing during pregnancy.

We chose to have faith. We trusted in the Lord. We aligned ourselves with God. We had courage, and we never gave up. We tried to live the way we believe, with trust and hope.

Some said, "Why baptize a baby?" They said it with indignation and incredulous words. We were offering Little Will to the Lord and putting our trust in the Lord. It's possible that Little Will could have died in utero, during a "procedure," at birth, or during any number of situations in those six months in the NICU. He did not. He could have died on the way to see Grandma and Grandpa, on the way to relocate across the country in the middle of nowhere. He did not.

Perhaps God is in this. What else is there? To not trust in the Lord is to lie down and die or to give up. What fun is that? I'm not always a good sport, but I'm mostly obedient. *Perhaps he'll die, but perhaps he'll live!* My lesson from this experience is this tag line: "We can get busy living, or we can get busy dying." To make this choice, we must have the courage to move. Perhaps we can overcome death with life. In our case, he gave our Little Will six years more than anyone expected, but we never doubted. God was in this.

Cathy Kilpatrick *is the CEO of Sunflower Ministries LLC and focuses on Splankna Therapy to help with PTSD, anxiety, depression, and pain. She connects people with their emotions where traditional talk therapy isn't quite enough. Cathy helps people become more than the lies they believe. Her motto is, "If we clear the traumas in our lives and dispel the lies we believe, we can be transformed." Contact Cathy at* **SunflowerMinistriesLLC.com** *or* **CathyAnn.Kilpatrick@gmail.com, 972.736.6513.**

Thoughts to Ponder

from Never Give Up

1. Don't give up when circumstances are overwhelming.

2. Your faith can encourage others.

3. With God, you will never be alone.

> **In difficult situations, how has your hope been strengthened?**

Be strong and take heart,
all you who hope in the Lord. — Psalm 31:24

In the Making

by Tobi Adeyemi

Throughout my life, God has chiseled my character, sometimes in unexpected ways. Thank God, I'm not a finished work yet. He continues to transform me—I'm still in the making.

When I was young, my dad was a seminary student and church pastor. Our daily and weekly routine included going to church, family prayers, and repeating Bible verses in the evening before bedtime. Memorizing Bible verses came easily to me. My first-grade Sunday school teacher gave me my first Adventure Bible. I loved hearing and reading Bible stories and pictured myself in the scenes. The "just for kids" notes helped simplify the stories, summarized main points, and outlined Christian doctrines. I was intrigued by the New Testament account of Jesus and His followers, such as Peter and Paul, who had courageous faith.

At the age of eight, while watching TBN's Kids' Club on a Saturday morning, I repeated a prayer to ask Jesus to forgive my sins, come into my heart, and be the Lord of my life. I was baptized at the age of nine in the home church my family attended. I had no doubts and fully believed the gospel message without question. I knew that Jesus loved the little children of the world, and I was captivated by images of starving children. I wanted to grow up to feed them and share Jesus with them. I also had a rising desire to share the gospel with friends in school. My first attempt to witness was to a friend in first grade. I asked if she wanted to go to Heaven. That did not go well, because life after death was not her main concern as we played outside during recess time.

I continued to be involved in Sunday school, VBS, and AWANA clubs as I progressed through my school years. In elementary and middle school, I was considered the quiet, nice, and smart girl who got along well with others, made good grades, and did not cause trouble.

Although I gained more knowledge about the Christian faith, there was turmoil at home and within my spirit. I was generally an observer, and with my Nigerian cultural heritage, there was the unstated expectation of not questioning authority. It seemed that most decisions were made by my dad, and I felt like I was being unfairly controlled. Over the years, bitterness and resentment took root, and I became guarded toward my parents and family. I felt confined, not being able to do what my friends got to do, feeling that no one understood me, and fearing discipline for not doing what I was supposed to do.

I still admired the heroes of faith. While in high school, I thought about career pursuits. I wanted to be a doctor or a missionary. It was hard for me to share what was on my heart or my emotions. Being quiet by nature, I became more withdrawn.

As I approached my last two years of high school, my dad neared the completion of his Ph.D.

Tension increased regarding my family staying in the United States or returning to Nigeria after he completed his degree. My parents decided I should graduate a year early from high school. I needed to take a few extra classes simultaneously, but I would indeed be able to complete my last two years of high school in one year. I was sad, because I would not be able to graduate with my true graduating class. I would have to attend a university that was not my first choice. I felt that I had no voice. At the same time, I wanted to leave home, and the university was my way out.

At seventeen years old, I entered the university in the fall of 2005 to pursue a bachelor's degree in biology, with the anticipation of following the pre-medicine route. I lived on campus for my first year and did not have transportation. However, since church and fellowship among believers had always been a part of my life, I wanted to be among the body of Christ. I did not want to do anything bad for fear of not living up to the expectation of a good child.

I attended an on-campus fellowship on Sunday mornings and went to Tuesday night Bible studies with the Baptist Student Ministry. I was part of a small accountability group with five to six other young ladies in my dorm. We met once a week and engaged in a small outreach in our dorm, taking out the trash for all the residents on our floors. Prayer for others and my life direction had a profound impact on me. I incorporated reading Scripture and devotionals. Journaling and quiet times were part of my spiritual routine. This kept me motivated and encouraged, despite frustration with classes, loneliness, and uncertainty about the future.

My parents decided to stay in the United States, and I spent the first summer after college at home with them. There was still unresolved tension within me, and I often did not want to speak with them. I wanted to be any place but home. Because feelings were not openly discussed, I had no way of expressing this, and I found refuge in writing, reading, and solitary activities. That summer, I landed a job in Aurora, Colorado. The moment I entered Colorado and saw the mountains, I felt a sense of freedom and resolved in my heart to move there, far from home. I talked with my aunt and uncle about this, because I felt they were more understanding than my parents. Over the years I attempted several times to move to Colorado, but my desire to relocate was never fulfilled.

In my second year of college, I decided I was not as interested in biology or becoming a doctor as I had thought. I became discouraged and fearful, not knowing what to do. I still wanted to be an overseas missionary but did not know what other major or profession could be utilized on the field. I cried out to God for direction and acknowledged that I had no idea what to do. I was frustrated and contemplated switching majors or attending a different university that had a Speech Pathology program. Plans were in place to transfer, but at the last moment, the housing situation for the new university fell through. Looking back, I believe that was the Lord's response to having me stay, because I had built relationships and established a community within the dorms.

In the following years in college, we began a weekly dorm-wide Bible study, and I attended church off-campus. I never claimed one church as a church home, but each week as I read the Word of God and listened to sermons, I saw that the Word of God was living and active, sharper than a double-edged sword. The scriptures that I had previously read took on a deeper, more relevant meaning. I discovered where my thoughts, motives, and actions stemmed from, and whether I lived in the image of God. I began to view the world from a different perspective and was saddened by how apathetic and

167

distant from God others seemed to be. I had an overwhelming fear to step out of my comfort zone juxtaposed to an overwhelming burden to share truth.

I felt inadequate and did not know how to go about broadcasting Christ to the whole world or get anyone to listen. I wanted to retreat and kept this struggle and burden inward. At the same time, I knew doubt and discouragement were not of God, and I was called to be a light, no matter where I was. My conclusion was that all I could do was pray. I held even tighter to prayer, especially by praying the Word of God.

I graduated from college in 2009 with a BA in Biology. I wanted to further my education in public health and establish health programs to serve the underserved. I wanted to "speak up for those who cannot speak for themselves, for the rights of all who are destitute" (Proverbs 31:8). I was accepted in a graduate Public Health program but declined at the last moment due to being advised to attend nursing school to broaden my career prospects. In the interim, I contemplated teaching and entered an alternative teaching certification program while taking prerequisites for admissions to nursing school.

Two years later, I was accepted into a nursing program. Nursing school was a test of faith and endurance. I was challenged to "not be anxious about anything, but in every situation, by prayer and petition, with thanksgiving, present your requests to God" (Philippians 4:6). I prayed daily and asked for the Lord to remove anxiety and bestow His favor. He answered my prayers. For the first time, I asked the Lord to change my heart toward my parents and family and to help me be a witness through my career.

Over time, as I continued to read the Word of God and dedicated more time with Him, I slowly released hurt and resentment toward others. I asked God to change my perspective. I gradually saw a difference in the way I related to my family. I prayed that God would reveal more things to me about my nature, the world, and the people He created. I also wanted to share His truth wherever I was and prayed for opportunities to do that.

I realized there were things that God would call me to do that I would not understand. Others might not think this was the way I should go, but I would have to follow where the Lord was leading me. I needed to learn to walk by faith, in step with Him. With a desire to be Christ-like, I saw my patterns change.

As I began my first nursing job, I felt a stirring within that this would not be the place I would settle. I was not sure what that meant or what it would look like. Six months later, I resigned from the position. I had no job lined up when I resigned, but I felt a peace that the Lord would be with me. Within a month, a new position opened in a different city, requiring me to move from home. The transition was smooth, and I spent time in the next position seeking the Lord and my life's direction.

During this season, I learned that as a child of God, I must be still before the Lord. He showed me things about His character. He gave me the strength to work under a manager, who was an atheist and did not want to hear about God. I worked at night and held to the promise in Psalm 18:28, "You, Lord, keep my lamp burning; my God turns my darkness into light." The time came for a new job opportunity in a different city, this time with a roommate.

Over the next year, I saw how hurt from my past had a profound impact on my relationships and interactions. I knew God was doing something new. To step into that, I needed to leave the past and what was comfortable and allow Him to chip away and refine hidden areas. I thought I had come to a place of being good, but as this race must be run with endurance, there was still plenty of work to be done. I listened to sermons that merged calling, purpose, Jesus, and faith. Living life intentionally for the sake of the call of Christ was the heartbeat of my days. I prayed for opportunities to minister to others and found that unexpected or divine encounters occurred. I was thrust into situations where I was actively speaking to others and applying the truth of what I was reading and learning in God's Word. I learned that the mind is a battlefield, prayer is powerful, and that the Word of God is strong enough to transform.

In 2014, I attended a church and became active in their young adult ministry. I wanted to grow and serve within the church, but I continually made excuses that I was planning to move and wanted to do outreach, so I did not follow through with serving. As time went on, I stopped attending young-adult gatherings. However, I met a friend who wanted to know God deeper and for us to pray together. This was something I had been looking for since college.

During the time we spent together, iron was sharpened, motives and intentions were challenged with the Word of God, and we asked God to pour His Spirit into us and make us sensitive to His prompting in our sphere of influences. Over the next two years, I studied the book of John, learned about the words that Jesus spoke, the lessons He taught, and the miracles He performed. In a fresh way, I learned that Jesus was God. I also spent time engaged in dedicated studies through books of the Bible relating to the church and godly living. I contemplated attending seminary so I would have the credentials and ethos to properly proclaim the message of Christ, if and when I wrote.

In 2016, I moved back into my parents' house, with another nudging in my spirit that this was a transitional season. I tried blogging and began with a few postings, which I shared with friends. I hesitated, not wanting to seem judgmental, wanting the words that I posted to be the truth and not my own opinion. This caused me to abandon my post.

I visited Colorado three times that year. The first time was a reawakening, with God reassuring me that He was the Sovereign God of my life. Every ability He had given me was to be used for His glory. I realized that He hears when I ask according to His will, and He answers. The second trip was a reminder of the need to share the truth with youth, the future generations, and that the world is hurting and longing to be loved. The third trip, God revealed the residual abandonment, self-sufficiency, and unworthiness still present in my life that needed to be surrendered to Him.

In the fall, I was allowed to work as a school nurse in a Title I school in my hometown—the school I attended as a child. The tides had turned, and my life had come full circle. I was back to the place where I learned so much about the God I served, and I knew this was an opportunity to share God's love for the children He created.

Each morning, a nurse from a different school and I prayed by phone for our campuses. At the end of the first semester, during a prayer time, the word image of camp came into my spirit. Since I would be off during the summer, I looked for youth camps. The search led to a job board posting for a program at a university in Raleigh, North Carolina. I was not sure the university existed, but went ahead and applied in February 2017, and left it in the Lord's hands. I told Him I was clearing my schedule and was willing to do whatever He wanted me to do. I would go wherever He wanted me to go.

In March 2017, I received a call and scheduled a FaceTime interview. A few days after the interview, I was offered the position and asked if I would be able to attend the required one-day orientation in Raleigh in April. Without hesitation, I confirmed that I would attend and booked a plane ticket, hotel room, and transportation.

When I arrived at Raleigh-Durham International airport, I believed that this city would become a place of growth for me. During the summer program, I was prompted to confront my fears of facing giants and take leaps of faith. With prayer, seeking the Lord's guidance in His Word, and receiving confirmation, I resigned from my school nurse position.

Back at home in Texas at the end of the summer, I continued to apply for jobs and had interviews for part-time positions that were last-ditch attempts to make some extra income. I even considered moving to Houston, but the weekend I was planning to go was the same weekend Hurricane Harvey made landfall. Yet again, I had to decide to stop striving with God and allow Him to be the One to move my steps.

In October, I took another leap of faith and attended a job fair in Durham, North Carolina. I met with two managers and told them I had come from Texas and was returning there in two days. I also found information about how to get my nursing license endorsed in North Carolina and began the process. As I boarded the plane to leave, one of the managers left a voice message offering me a position, which I accepted.

The next month I moved from Texas to North Carolina. Upon arrival, I found out the job was offered verbally, not officially through Human Resources. I wondered if I had made the wrong decision. I later realized the time spent in waiting until the paperwork was complete and authorized was crucial, as

I had to lean into the Lord. The discomfort in my life reinforced my dependence on Him. I could do nothing in my strength. I had a renewed desire to share what God was teaching me. I hoped to encourage the faith of other believers.

I am continually challenged in my faith that God alone equips, supplies, and provides. He is the One who will fight for me, and He is the God of angel armies, who goes before me. I must not rely on my ability, my finances, or material resources. He will bring the people and the resources I need to complete the task He sets before me so that He gets the glory.

While I am in the making, I have also seen the reasons God's Word is perfect, and why His wisdom should be heeded. It keeps us from hurt, transforms us, enables us to encourage, instruct, and correct, and points people ultimately toward His love and renown. God is continually revealing Himself, and if we are open and ask, He makes known His wisdom. We may plan our ways, but God knows the plans He has for us and orchestrates them to draw us into closer fellowship with Him. For all His goodness, I am grateful to be continually in the making.

Tobi Adeyemi *was raised in Mesquite, Texas. She claims roots to Maryland and Nigeria, having been born in Washington, D.C. to Nigerian parents. Tobi is the third born of four children. She has worked as a Registered Nurse since 2012. Apart from writing inspirational pieces and jotting down quotable notables and taglines, Tobi enjoys scenic skyscapes, going on runs, striking up sporadic conversations, and working with children and youth. Tobi is also a self-acclaimed muffin aficionado (baking and tasting). View Tobi's blogs at* **UrbanPauseWeb.wordpress.com** *and* **Tobi316Blog.wordpress.com.** *Email Tobi at* **Tobi316Blog@gmail.com.**

Thoughts to Ponder

from In the Making

1. God reveals truth when you seek Him with your whole heart.

2. Bitterness and resentment can take root if left unchecked.

3. God orchestrates events to bring you closer to Him.

> **What situations has God used to transform you?**

And we all, who with unveiled faces contemplate the Lord's glory, are being transformed into His image with ever-increasing glory. — 2 Corinthians 3:18

Finding Peace in War
by Lara Lorena Cardoso Zwahlen

Nestled in what should have been a safe mother's womb, I did not find peace. Anxiety and war filled my mother's life, causing great fear and sickness. I was born two weeks early, weighing only three pounds. My parents, who were married the previous year, were Portuguese colonists living in Angola, Africa. They had come from broken homes and hoped for a new and better life together. Angola offered them a treasure of memories—"golden years." Unfortunately, a civil war had begun. The communists fueled the war and brainwashed the natives to attack the colonists. They wanted to take over the rich resources of coffee, oil, and diamonds. Our peace was vandalized.

As a little girl, I should not have witnessed death outside my bedroom window, but I did. Men shot at one another on the street below. Afterward, while walking in our neighborhood, I played with the bullet casings. I thought we were safe in our home on the ninth floor of a tall high-rise apartment building. However, one day my sister and I fearfully hid under my bed while our mother ran across the street for groceries. While she was away, men with guns raided our building. We heard loud pounding and rough voices shouting and screaming. Our tall building was not a safe fortress after all.

Miraculously, my mother returned and frantically gathered some clothes into a suitcase. She ran away with us. The threat was imminent: Portuguese colonists were hunted and killed.

"Where was your father?" you ask. He was a Commanding Officer in the Portuguese military, fighting guerrilla warfare in the jungle. Later, he joined us. We left in a state of panic, and refugees were forced to leave or risk death. We left everything behind, yet managed to escape unscathed by obtaining a secure flight to Portugal. In the ensuing months, the entire country of Angola became a cauldron of misery and death.

Portugal could not provide my father with a job since the country was in the middle of a recession, so my mother encouraged him to apply for visas to America. In the meantime, we traveled to France. As we waited for our visas to process, we visited our relatives on my mother's side. Riots arose in Portugal. Miraculously, we were granted visas within three months. We were truly thankful for all the gracious people who helped us. Finally, we would find peace from the war in this new land called America.

We arrived in America just like the first pilgrims, in search of freedom and a better life. My mother was in line, waiting to go through customs, while my father held mine and my sister's hands. Distracted, my father briefly let go of our hands.

Unknown to him, an old lady with tantalizing candy lured my sister and me away. She gave us one piece at a time until we turned around and didn't recognize anyone or anything. We were frightened. No one spoke our language. *Who is this old lady? At least my sister and I have each other.* The war was still fresh in our minds, and we were experiencing fear and danger again.

The authorities were notified, and they searched the airport for hours with no success. They politely told our parents the sad news and asked them to go to their home. They said, "Your little daughters are gone forever, probably on another flight abroad." My mother was gripped with despair and unbelief. In an elevator, along with my father, she sobbed and cried out in Portuguese, "Deus, ajuda mi," which means, "God, help me."

A rather tall man standing behind her turned and asked in their Portuguese language how he could help them. My mother thought he was an angel from Heaven. He explained that he was from Brazil, so he could understand Portuguese. He asked for a description of us. My mother explained that we looked like little boys with short dark hair, wearing boy clothes, but we were girls. He asked if the authorities had looked on a floor where construction was taking place. My parents didn't know. He assured them he would personally look there, and no one would suspect him. He found us with the old lady. He must have befriended her, because he said, "May I help take the little boys to the men's bathroom?" She then allowed him to do so.

This gave us a safe distance to escape. We celebrated our reunion with a trip to McDonald's, where we ate our first American burger. We had heard so much about this special food that I'm sure, like the pilgrims, we gave thanks to God. We were not sure if America was a safe and peaceful place to live, but we were thankful to be away from the conflict of the civil war.

Perhaps we would find refuge once we were settled into our new home. The first year in America, my great uncle on my mother's side was our sponsor. We experienced our first snowfall. It was a magical winter wonderland. I started kindergarten that year at the local elementary school and learned English quickly. We were thankful to have a Portuguese relative help us during our transition. Regrettably, he was a divorced, lonely old man. He encouraged my parents to go on dates and leave us with him. What seemed like an innocent gift to my parents became dysfunctional molestation for me. Again, I thought I was safe, but a conflict arose in my young heart. Part of my innocence was stolen, yet I kept this secret until my teens. I was grateful that we moved before they raped me.

My father seemed to always be upset and frustrated. I rationalized that his anger was due to the difficult circumstances we faced, especially since he had a tough time finding work. Finally, he was able to join the armed forces, which was familiar to him. He had been a high-ranking officer in the Portuguese army in Angola, Africa, but here in America, nothing transferred over. He started at the bottom as a private at thirty-two years of age. This was a hard and humbling experience, and he said he only made it through basic training because he didn't understand the swear words yelled at him by his drill sergeant.

By working two jobs, my mother played a huge part in helping him. Times were difficult during this season. My parents fought all the time. They warred with their tongues against each other. My father's rage flared up at times, and he beat my mother into silence. The war within our household took a toll on my mind and heart. My sister and I were terrified of my father, and our relationship with him was estranged. We never knew when he would blow up in anger.

Providentially, a sweet elderly lady constantly bought us extra groceries for us from the military grocery store, called the commissary. My mother was a cashier there and developed a relationship with her when she regularly came to shop. This lovely lady invited us to her church one Sunday, and we attended. I was hopeful that change would occur in our home through our new community of support. Living in a low-income

176

neighborhood presented many opportunities for us to trust God. We committed our lives to follow Jesus and were all baptized at our new-found church community.

During this season, our grandma, Avo Fatima, came from Portugal to visit us for several months. She made homemade meals from scratch. She brought such a fragrance of peace and love into our home. My father never beat my mother whenever my grandma came to visit. Our lives were shifting to a peaceful state, or so we thought.

As soon as my grandma left, the war flared up its ugly head. My father began beating my mother again. We were also beaten when we tried to help her. One summer day, our cat delivered a litter of cute kittens. If our parents were at work, my sister and I were not allowed outside, and no one was ever allowed inside our home. Nevertheless, we decided to ignore the rules and sneaked our friends into our home to see the kittens. It seemed harmless.

The mother cat did not care for visitors touching her babies. She scared us with her growl and hissed with discontentment. To our surprise, she even bit one of our friends, drawing blood. The child ran home crying. Later that evening, the child's mother decided to confront my parents about the situation, but only my father was home. I witnessed my father turning shades of red as the furious mother yelled at him. I wanted to hide, but I was paralyzed with fear. We received lashes by his belt all over our naked bodies. I was humiliated, and my soul was crushed. When I went to school days later with those marks visible, everyone turned a blind eye. We never spoke of the war or dysfunction in our home. We simply swept it under a rug and put on fake smiles. This confused me profusely, because we attended church the following Sunday.

In addition to my physical wounds, there was a huge void in my heart. I tried to fill it, which led to tremendous trouble and terrible choices. Prejudice affected me throughout my upper elementary years. I was a foreigner—an alien. We finally gained our citizenship as Americans when I was a pre-teen.

When my father was assigned to military bases abroad, we were given a fresh start in different countries. As a middle schooler in Germany, bullies often targeted me, and I avoided them or hid. During my high school years in Italy, I looked for love in all the wrong places. I welcomed the beautiful distractions this country offered, along with a couple of serious relationships with guys at my school. With their empty promises of love, they left me even more wounded.

The pinnacle of my fear occurred one afternoon when we were alone with my father. A conflict arose. My father yelled at me about how I spent my time, constantly involved in outside relationships rather than being at home. I had become completely rebellious toward my parents and abandoned any morals I once valued.

I yelled a curse word at my father. He became enraged and attacked me, hitting me blow after blow with his fists. Thankfully, my sister appeared, pushing him away from me. Eventually, my mother was contacted, and they rushed me to the Italian hospital. I had to lie about what happened. If I told the truth, my father might have been jailed and lost his job. Out of fear, I swallowed the whole painful event and never brought it up again.

I began questioning who God was. *Why was my life filled with war and pain?* I didn't trust God or any man. My soul and mind were at war with each other. Since my heart was broken and crushed, I didn't know what to believe. *How could a loving God allow such pain and suffering? Who could I ever trust? How could I find peace in this world?*

I determined to fix my problems on my own. I didn't need a God who was furious with me like my father was. I vowed to self-protect my wounds. However, a war raged in the pit of my soul. A violent, corrupt cesspool of bitterness toward my father consumed me. I was angry with God and all mankind. From my heart and out of my mouth, a vile cynical poison poured out. Fear gripped me at night. Because I was afraid something horrific would happen, days passed when I did not sleep. An evil presence tried to imprison me with paralyzing fear. Betrayal played repeatedly in my mind, plaguing me with misery and no hope for a future. But God met me in that war pit of pain, fear, and betrayal.

Through a sequence of events, I was invited to attend a new Christ-following church. I was discipled and held accountable by

178

loving, genuine people. This group of Christ-followers accepted me from my ugly cesspool. Over time, I came to realize that God is compassionate, slow to anger, abounding in love, and a faithful Father. I didn't just know *about* Him, I came to personally know God as my loving Father, Jesus as my best friend, and the Holy Spirit as my guide. As I began to study the Bible, God in three-parts-together-as-one romanced my heart with unconditional love. The truth renewed my mind.

A tremendous amount of lies kept me bound with chains and held me back from who I truly was. Over time, I identified the lies and replaced them with the truth. Through prayer and faith, different churches and people helped me battle the fear. In my faith journey, the greatest truths I found were that God loved me as I was, and His perfect love casts away all fear. When it became clear to me how vast yet personal His love was toward me, I finally rested in His loving arms in complete peace. Fear no longer had a hold on my life. Instead, I experienced the presence of God by intentionally inviting Jesus into every part of my life.

Years later, Jesus called me to ministry. For me to receive healing, He needed to address things in my heart. The first one was between God and me. My heart was deceitful at times, allowing doubt to rob my trust in God. But in seeking His truth, I came to know that God gives free choice to all people. In this broken world, wounded people hurt others with their poor choices. God forgave me and washed me of those hidden lies. I wanted more of God so I could make a difference in this suffering world.

As I gained a better understanding of God's intent, I allowed the Great Physician Jesus to heal my heart of deep, infected wounds. Even though I had become a Christian, it took a long time. Painfully, but necessary for healing, Jesus reopened my wounds by taking me back to the painful places. As I recalled these events, almost like on a movie screen, each scenario appeared before me. Only this time, I saw Jesus holding me ever so close to His heart, and He was crying over me. I felt waves of His love wash over me again and again. Exhilarating joy filled my heart.

My transformation was not yet complete. Jesus then asked

me to forgive my father and let my bitterness go. I wrestled for months over Jesus' request. Courage came as I worshiped the Lord and constantly kept His Word before me. I faced my father not long afterward, and said, "I forgive you for beating me and our family all of those years."

He just looked at me with a dazed look and said, "I don't know what you are talking about."

I started to get angry, but a wave of love came over me, and I saw my father as a little wounded child inside of his adult body. Each day I reminded myself of that until I believed it: *I forgive you, Dad. I forgive you, Father. I forgive you, Pai.*

My whole life turned around because of this encounter with God the Father, Jesus His Son, the Holy Spirit, and my biological father. A couple of years later, after I processed my pain through Bible studies, God called me to a prison ministry, where I shared my story with eighty female inmates. They all understood my pain. The Lord gave me many opportunities to bring hope to them through a relationship with Jesus and healing prayer. Then He called me to youth groups and women's ministries. He brought truth and healing to them through His abounding love.

In my journey with the Lord, new revelations became realities. God turned my pain-filled life into a message of hope. He turned my tests into testimonies and my trials into triumphs. Instead of being a victim of war, I became a victor.

Each day, I envision myself nestled safely in my Heavenly Father's arms. I know Him as my Prince of Peace, Jesus Christ. He drives away all fear in my heart and mind through His everlasting love toward me. I can completely rest in Him. When I trust Him by surrendering my will and circumstances to Him, He brings true peace. A whisper of His Holy Spirit confirms the truth in my spirit. I am His beloved and protected treasure. There in His loving arms, I rest in complete peace each day.

May you come to know this peace.

Lara Zwahlen, daughter of the Prince of Peace, wife, mother, grandmother, author, artist, former educator, Bible study teacher and coordinator, and a civil war survivor. She was born a colonist during a civil war in Angola, Africa, then escaped to America as a child. She is a conduit for Christ through the vehicles of painting, healing prayer, and biblical truth. She is also a board member for Higher than I ministry. Please feel free to contact Lara for more information about her book, From War to Warrior, *and resources about prayer, healing, and freedom from fear.* **HigherThanI@gmail.com.**

Thoughts to Ponder

from Finding Peace in War

1. The Holy Spirit helps you identify the lies you believe.

2. Meditating on scriptural truth enables you to replace Satan's lies.

3. You must forgive others before you can fully heal.

How can you experience peace instead of war?

Peace I leave with you; My peace I give you. I do not give to you as the world gives. Do not let your hearts be troubled and do not be afraid. — John 14:27

Sink or Swim

by Diane Claire

Have you ever swum through life's challenges doing the backstroke, frantically dog-paddling? Or maybe you didn't even know how to swim. When I was betrayed by my husband, I felt like I was drowning, unable to surface for a breath. *How did this happen? Where do I go from here? How do I get out of this dilemma? I am drowning, Lord. Please help me!*

I found myself drowning in an awful abyss—sinking to the depths of despair. Many people tried to help and advise me, based on their own experiences. They said, "Leave him or throw him out. Take your children away from everyone and start a new life." Or "A wife should never leave. Stay with him. Endure it. Stick it out. He will change." Or "You made your bed, now lie in it. You married him, now deal with it." You know—all the clichés of life. Through the comfort of my family and friends, I just wanted the pain to go away. However, they did not have the answers. Therefore, I tried to sort everything out in *my* strength.

I grew up in a traditional family home and was the oldest of four siblings. My mom and dad loved each other, and we faithfully attended church every Sunday. In our small town, Mom and Dad participated as coaches and leaders in various events. We were involved in Girl Scouts, baseball, basketball, and ballet.

Both of my parents came from families of ten siblings. Mom was a country girl, and Dad was a city boy. My dad and his brothers were cooks and bakers. Even at family gatherings, the men cooked, and the women cleaned the kitchen. What a role reversal. Come to think of it, in my family, women cleaned up after their men in many different ways. Oh, the memories. I can smell the fresh pastries now—fresh pies, cakes, and bread. Yum!

I thank God that my dad cooked, because when he was away from home, my mom never prepared meals. She served a slice of bologna between two pieces of bread and a glass of milk, expecting us to be satisfied.

Family gatherings were noisy and fun. My aunts, uncles, and cousins played relay games with all the kids and sometimes acted crazy. In many families, you have that "special aunt or uncle." For me, that was my great-aunt Cleo. Although she was quiet, she had a positive attitude and a peace that I never quite understood. I liked her smile and her tender touch.

At age twenty, I married a public servant who was abusive. I understood and accepted the weird hours and the stress he had on the job. He gave his all at work. However, he was never there to take care of me and our precious daughters. I later found out he was having affairs instead of working overtime as he claimed. My dreams of having the same family life as I had experienced with my mom and dad were shattered. I was drowning.

My husband came home one afternoon and told me he was moving out to live with his mother until I "grew up." Speechless, my mind started to spin, and I had nothing to say. I couldn't imagine him living with his mother until I "grew up."

Who would help provide for our daughters? He was the man of the house who was supposed to financially support his family. *What would I do when he was no longer in the picture? To whom could I turn?*

After we divorced, I was unsure of what to do with my life. My daughters were two and six years old. They enjoyed playing and being little girls. I was concerned about the effect of them growing up in a single-parent home. I avoided letting them see me cry and hit my pillow at night. I believed that everything was my fault—from the physical and verbal abuse to the affairs with other women. I was convinced I could have prevented this if I had tried harder to make him happy. All these thoughts depressed me, creating guilt and low self-esteem.

Where do I go? No one understands.

When people looked at me, I felt like they saw me wearing a big D for divorce. I thought they viewed my husband as a public servant and a pillar of the community, while I was not the wife I should have been. *Yes, we divorced, but I did not have the affair. He did. Why do I feel guilty like I am a nobody?*

One day I decided to enter a cathedral that I had passed many times. *Maybe the church would be my answer.* As I hesitantly entered the sanctuary, every footstep echoed. The statues seemed to follow my every move. I asked God, *Why am I here? Why am I alive? Who am I? What am I going to do? I'm drowning!*

As I walked down the aisle of this huge ornate cathedral, I sat in the front pew with tears streaming down my face. The silent echo of my thoughts and questions was overwhelming. With such big responsibilities, I did not know how I was going to get through the minutes, days, and years ahead. My daughters needed me, and I knew deep inside that I would be their only provider. Sobbing, I knelt and begged God to take control of my life. I prayed, *I need you, God, to take control of my life.*

Calmness came over me, a feeling I had never experienced before. Was it the result of my sincere plea for God to take over my life? I did not fully understand what had just happened, but I felt at peace. I had no idea how my life would be better, but I knew it would. *Why am I feeling this peace within?* The relief felt good.

My new life was filled with reading and studying the Bible, which I had never done before. I was eager to try new things in my life. A friend invited me to a women's Bible study. Nervously, I walked into the room with women sitting at a long table. Immediately, I recognized a familiar face, my great aunt Cleo. She stood and announced to the group, "This is my niece, whom we have been praying for." I was amazed, because I thought no one prayed for me. *Who would want to pray for me? I'm a nothing.* As I looked at the ladies, they nodded, accepting me with peaceful smiles. For the entire hour, I was confused by the startling question, *Why would these ladies pray for me?*

The pastor and his wife sat beside me as everyone was leaving. Pastor Bill told me that they knew my story from Aunt Cleo and would like to help. Over and over, I told them it was my problem and no one could help. Pastor Bill calmly said, "Let's see what God has to say about this situation."

What? God has something to say? Not my Mom, Dad, friends, or the church . . . but God? I wish I could remember everything that was said that night, but what I do remember is 2 Corinthians 5:17. "Therefore, if anyone is in Christ, the new creation has come: The old has gone, the new is here!" This was the first time I heard this scripture, and it was comforting.

My daughters and I attended church services several Sundays before I made my profession of faith public. The day I publicly dedicated my life to Christ, I felt the same peace as I had felt in the cathedral on that lonely day when I asked God to take control of my life. Everyone in church that morning was accepting and loving. One lady came to me, held my hand, and said, "Remember, God does not teach you how to swim to drown you." My new life statement!

As weeks passed, my confidence sank to an all-time low. Some days, my newly found faith was strong, bringing great peace, but at other times, I lost momentum and strength. *Lord, how am I going to provide for my daughters and me?* With no college education, I knew my prospects for a good-paying job were non-existent.

My mom continued to say, "To be somebody, you should be married." Should I start dating and find a husband—going from the proverbial frying pan to the fire? Did being divorced make me a "nobody?" So many questions and doubts. My biggest concern was how to continue with my life and not make the same mistakes.

I learned more about my new way of life from church services and Bible studies. I discovered that God shows us His plan one step at a time. It's like being a wanderer in the dark, who holds a lantern that reveals light for each new step. When you least expect it, God places someone in your life to be a helper and guide. You pray and listen for the still small voice to guide you in the direction God wants you to go.

The person God placed in my life suggested that the local community college could be a great place to start. I had never thought of that as an option. In the small town where I grew up, the teachers and counselors who knew my mom and dad held only an eighth-grade education. I felt fortunate to have graduated from high school. No one ever encouraged me to further my education so I could provide for myself. The big question was how could I pay for college? It was an impossible dream.

A friend and I visited the registrar in the community college admissions office. She suggested I take computer courses to attain a degree in computer science. At that time, I had no idea what a computer looked like or how it worked. I didn't even know algebra or geometry.

I was accepted into the Computer Science program, and the state supplied college grants to pay for my courses. My oldest daughter started first grade at the neighborhood school. My dad was supportive and provided after-school transportation and care. My younger daughter went to the daycare on campus. What a relief that I did not have to worry about my daughters' care.

I was excited to attend college full-time. The idea of going on welfare was not in my plans. I did not want to rely on the government to provide for my daughters and me, but there were no other financial options available. I chose to swallow my pride and use this means to help me achieve my goal. I thought welfare was for helping single moms provide for their families while pursuing their careers. At the welfare office, I explained my plan and asked for assistance for two-and-a-half years. I was surprised to learn that there was no time limit for assistance. The reality of a dream I had never thought possible was soon to change my life. God worked out all my steps, from getting grants and scholarships to providing financial support. Once again, God was faithful. "God does not teach you how to swim to drown you."

My first class was creative writing. As I looked around the room, everyone was fresh out of high school. My first class assignment was to write a paper on, "What do I want to be when I grow up?" I found that funny, because I thought I was "grown up." I realized I had embarked on a new adventure of raising two daughters while attending college.

I pondered the topic, "What do I want to be when I grow up?" I pictured my life as a wife and mother, owning a house with a large back yard. I certainly did not want to be a single mom. I always thought a couple would enjoy life together and have a loving relationship like my parents. My dream was now shattered.

My next class was computer programming. Without knowing what a computer looked like or how it worked, I was expected to program one in basic code. I discovered that programming was just like raising children. You must give them complete instructions for the simplest task.

Attending school full-time and raising two daughters was not easy. Throughout the years attending college, my ex-husband obtained my school schedule. He scheduled court dates during the times I had exams. I was blessed to have professors who understood and gave me tests the day before or after so I could complete my course work. This abusive behavior was another way my ex-husband used to harass and frustrate me.

By the grace of God, I completed my Associates of Science degree in Computer Science. I was the first in my family to graduate from college. On graduation day, I was so excited to see my daughters sitting by Mom and Dad. This was the moment in my life when I "grew up."

A few weeks after graduation, I was informed that I had to move out of my house. My dream house with the large yard and picket fence was taken away by my ex-husband. He wanted us out of the house, and it did not matter where we would live. *Where could I go?* With my degree, I finally had confidence in myself and knew God was working in my life. I wanted to move on with my life and watch my daughters grow up in a better environment. But where?

It amazes me that we meet people every day and never realize that they could be angels sent by God. A family friend, who had moved to Dallas, was that angel. She invited me to start a new life away from the harassment I experienced in previous years. If I stayed in my hometown, it would never end. I had nothing to lose. With much prayer, I decided to take a giant "leap of faith" and move to Dallas. As a result of never receiving child support, I sold my furniture to pay for our plane tickets. With $400 cash, we were on our way to Texas.

The day we left for our new life was heart-wrenching for me, my daughters, and my parents, because we were moving so far away. After all, the girls and my parents were close. I knew this was my most important decision ever, and I needed to trust God and have faith to follow His plan. I experienced the same peaceful feeling as when I cried out to the Lord in that cathedral, asking God to take control of my life.

Now, thirty years later, my daughters and I still live in Texas. My prayers to see my daughters grown up in a better environment were answered. We have been blessed with God's provision throughout the years—more than I could have imagined. The girls were involved in swimming, ice skating, softball, flute, and violin lessons. They participated in choir mission trips and summer camps that led to many lifelong friendships. Both daughters graduated from college and are wonderful Christian women who volunteer with many ministries. My oldest daughter graduated from Texas A&M University and is a successful business professional living in Dallas. My youngest daughter graduated from Hardin Simmons University and is a successful government administrator and is married to a fine Christian man. I am enjoying my grandson, who was born and is being raised in Texas.

My professional career as a computer specialist has grown since my first day in the computer science lab. Now I know more about computers than I had ever expected to know. I own a home that is more than my dreams could imagine. My ministry is serving as director for a ladies' Sunday school class. They are my sisters in Christ, closest friends, and family. My "leap of faith" to move to Dallas is one of the best decisions I ever made. Through the years, the Lord has always been faithful. I swam, backstroked, dog-paddled, and even floated, but I never drowned. The most important lesson I learned was to trust God and know that "God does not teach you to swim to drown you" and "with God all things are possible" (Matthew 19:26).

Diane Claire has served as Director of a ladies' Bible fellowship class at Prestonwood Baptist Church for over twenty-five years. Through fellowship and the study of His Word, she and these ladies strive to grow in faith through a closer relationship with Christ. For three years, she also served on the board at the Family Pregnancy Center in Lewisville, Texas. Until her retirement, Diane worked as a Documentation Specialist/Technical Engineer. She also loves staging homes, traveling, and appreciates being able to spend time with her daughters, son-in-law, and grandson. Contact her at DianeClairePT@gmail.com.

Thoughts to Ponder

from Sink or Swim

1. Your path is directed by God one step at a time.

2. God can bring you confidence in the midst of confusion.

3. Jesus believes in you even when you don't believe in yourself.

What is God teaching you through difficult situations?

With God all things are possible. — Matthew 19:26

Seasons of Change
by Cherie Nichols

In this journey called life, transitions occur that change us forever. We move from one season to another, sometimes with great difficulty. Through these transitions, we learn to embrace our circumstances, and in the end, become better for it. These life transitions are called "seasons of change."

As a second-grader, I dreamed of becoming a special-education teacher. As one who had a mild learning disability, I wanted to help others with their disabilities. This would be my passion, my mission in life, and I would retire as a seventy-year-old teacher. Later I became an elementary teacher and have loved every moment of all the years I have taught.

From the age of two, and due to hereditary conditions, I experienced many medical difficulties. These health challenges were all being well-controlled with medications. However, at the age of forty-three, things changed.

I had successful lumbar fusion surgery, but afterward, I experienced weird physical symptoms that were unexplained. They included dizziness, trouble swallowing, and laryngitis. Being a teacher and having laryngitis do not go together. Additional random symptoms began, such as numbness in my right arm, vertigo with stabbing headaches, neck pain, hearing issues, and tripping for no reason. I tripped at my job and home and even fractured my elbow from one of the falls.

The symptoms rarely flared up at the same time. To top it off, I was tired a lot, but what elementary teacher is not? Remedy . . . I'd nap when I was able. Sometimes my symptoms were so bad they required an emergency room (ER) visit. I was always sent home with no diagnosis as soon as my symptoms were relieved. I had no extended-stay visits. I did not understand these things, but God knew what He was doing.

Many of these symptoms were mild and sporadic, so they were brushed off as anxiety. As a result, the doctors said, "Here's another prescription." The symptoms were always random and never lasted longer than I could tolerate. My solution was to grip the classroom counter, breathe, and say,

"I'll be fine in a moment." The reasons they gave were stress, anxiety, or a sinus infection.

My loving husband was always there with me—a doctor visit here, a doctor visit there. I had panic attacks that were attributed to stress and made random middle-of-the-night ER visits. There were never too many symptoms at one time. I was always dismissed after getting my blood checked and my blood pressure down. Nothing ever came back abnormal. Always no rhyme or reason. God knew what He was doing.

I eventually saw a neurologist, who tested me once again. After the test results were back, he ruled out the possibility of Multiple Sclerosis and seizures. He then sent me for a swallow test to check my neuromuscular capabilities in my esophagus. The results showed some weakness, so the doctor gave me a prescription for neuropathy pain. I knew that through this season, God was the only One in control and that He knew what He was doing.

Meanwhile, I continued to teach with these symptoms, knowing something wasn't right. In August 2015, my husband and I moved to Texas to help my dad and ailing mother. With my husband's salary, it was a blessing that I did not need to get a teaching job right away. The 2015–2016 school year was the first in seventeen years straight of teaching that I wasn't in the classroom. This made me extremely uncomfortable. I felt like I was out of the will of my destiny, for which I worked my entire life to achieve. I was losing my independence, but surely, I'd get it back.

It was wonderful to assist my mom and dad with their health needs, and even though I did not have a teaching job, I was thankful for the time to search for answers to all the symptoms that were plaguing me. Through this new season of change, God knew what He was doing.

I developed new symptoms. Instead of being tired all the time, I switched to never being physically or mentally sleepy. I went days and nights without sleeping. Other symptoms got worse. I was able to find a new primary physician, who referred me to a new, wonderful neurologist. The neurologist sent me for a cranial magnetic resonance imaging (MRI) scan, even though previous MRIs showed nothing alarming. He gave me the typical seizure tests, such as electroencephalogram (EEG), and all results were within the normal range, except for some neuropathy. There was still no firm diagnosis.

During this time, I attended a women's weekly Bible study group through my church. I met women who were prayer warriors and became lifelong friends. Being a part of this group allowed me to see that God was on my side through all my difficulties. God placed these amazing ladies in my life, because He knew I needed them. They listened to me and prayed over me when we were together. We laughed and cried together. I could be real with them. I texted them in the middle of many nights, asking for prayer. These godly women were my support system and showed true unconditional love.

My nights were excruciatingly painful. You know, the kind where they say, "What's your pain level on a scale of one to ten?" Mine was an eight or nine. Again, there were ER visits. Each time after they diagnosed me with another panic attack or high blood pressure, I was discharged when my blood pressure was back to normal.

There were nights that I cried out to God to take me. My husband would be sound asleep while I sat or curled up in the fetal position on the floor. I was wide awake for hours, mentally exhausted, in tears, and utterly frustrated. I felt defeated. Sometimes I called on God. Other times I just counted the seconds, the minutes, the hours till the sun came up and I thought, *No, I'm not leaving Earth today.*

In December 2016, in the middle of another sleepless night, I felt a sharp, stabbing pain behind my left eye. I decided it was time, again, to make an appointment with the neurologist. I prayed through the night and called my neurologist the next morning. They immediately fast-tracked me to do another cranial MRI at an offsite imaging center.

Within twenty-four hours, I got the dreaded call from the doctor that I needed to come in as soon as possible. This was during the holidays, and I told them I had a women's Bible study luncheon that I desperately wanted to attend. Their response was, "Go, but come straight here afterward" for the results. Forever etched in my mind, I sat in the room with my husband, when the nurse practitioner opened the door and said,

"You've had a stroke."

I had an ischemic stroke in my lower left cerebellum at the age of forty-six. All the symptoms that I had been experiencing were building up to a stroke. They said the stroke most likely happened within the week before the last MRI. *But I was functioning. What?* Strokes I know about take people down—"in the hospital" down. That sharp pain I felt behind my eye was a post-stroke symptom. I had not even gone to the hospital.

I was told I was "too young" to have this happen. Of course, I was too young. I had a teaching career. I had a calling to get back to. I was supposed to retire as a schoolteacher at the age of seventy, remember?

After finding out this news, my neurologist wanted more blood work for testing of autoimmune and blood disorders. There were more pieces to the "puzzle" that were needed beyond determining that it was a "stroke." They discovered a genetic blood clotting disorder that I had all my life. It was dangerous, if not controlled, especially after a stroke or any kind of clotting episode. Part of the additional puzzle pieces was that the numerous surgeries I had over the prior forty-six years were extremely dangerous with this condition, because blood thinners were needed.

Clotting was the culprit that sent me into the ischemic stroke, caused by Factor V Leiden. It was a relatively new genetic blood clotting disorder, with no known cure. The only choice was to be on blood thinners and baby aspirin for the rest of my life.

I prayed for answers for years, and my friends prayed that I'd get relief. The search for "What is this?" was over in January 2017. There were a couple of months of outpatient physical therapy and finding the right medications to keep clotting at bay.

Having an extensive list of medical issues, I was God-blessed with the ability to figure out what was wrong, through a mild health scare, and gain answers to why He allowed me to have my stroke. God knew what He was doing, and He gave me answers.

I was told by God, through other Christian women, that I needed to move from the "season" I was in, to a new season. *What? I lost the ability to do the job that I loved and knew I was called by God to do. Why, God, why?* I lost my comfort zone, my independence, my life, my love. I lost my heart, my passion, my mission.

This is not what I chose. Would anyone choose this? It wasn't my choice, but it happened. Although the damage from the stroke was mild in comparison to what it could have been, it was enough to change my career path. I cried and was scared. This was a "season of change," but by faith, I knew God knew what He was doing and would see me through.

People asked, "Was it an easy transition since it was a mild stroke?" Easy transition? Oh, my gosh, no! This has been the hardest part of my life's journey. Seven years later, I'm still trying to figure it out. Some days, I think I can conquer the world. Other days, I'm brought to my knees, lying on the floor, face down. My husband knows my stubbornness. So does God. Both know that I have a hard time gauging how much I can do at any given time. Now I must also figure out what I'm supposed to do and how to use my remaining abilities. Even with my stubbornness, I continue to seek what God put on my heart to do in this "post-disability" season.

In the summer of 2017, on a whim, I emailed the director of a nearby nonprofit Christian ministry. Looking back, I know God was constantly, but quietly, whispering to me about nonprofit ministries and placing them on my heart. I filled out a volunteer application. I told my ladies group that I felt God was calling me toward the nonprofit sector, and teaching was not going to be my lifelong calling after all.

God opened the door for me to volunteer and brought me to a place where my heart and soul have happiness on a weekly basis. I have even had a season of part-time work at a ministry I previously volunteered at. God has also allowed me to work in a classroom as a substitute teacher. I have the best of both worlds. I'm part of the best women's home group through my church, my support group. I also attend a Bible study group of older women through a local Bible study ministry. I've met more incredible women of God.

It is only through God's comfort that I am able to continue forward, even if, at times, it is on my knees. I cannot imagine what a non-believer of Jesus Christ would go through with my scenario. It's crushing to have to give up your life's passion or love. But for a believer, faith brings you to your knees. If you are going through a difficult time, find refuge and strength in your Savior, listen to the Holy Spirit, and cling to the Word of God. Meditate on Him and His Word. Have friends pray with you and for you. God will give you direction and answers in His time, not yours. Have faith that God will lead you through the next "season of change."

Cherie Nichols *was raised in North Texas. Currently, she lives in Allen, Texas, with her husband of ten years. She also has two cats. She recently started writing about her stroke story. In 2018, she was chosen as a finalist in her college alumni magazine, for her Q and A. It was published through John Brown University. She is determined to bring light to the genetic blood clotting disorder, Factor V Leiden. She wishes to help and encourage others to cope with and heal from the circumstances they are experiencing. In Cherie's spare time, when her body allows it, she loves a good geocaching hunt.*

Thoughts to Ponder
from Seasons of Change

1. God always knows what He is doing.

2. Each season of your life is another opportunity to grow in faith.

3. God will lead, nourish, protect, and restore you.

> **What is God doing for you during this season of your life?**

He has made everything beautiful in its time. He has also set eternity in the human heart; yet no one can fathom what God has done from beginning to end. — Ecclesiastes 3:11

Breaking the Rules
by Connie Steindorf

Are you a rule keeper or a rule breaker? I've heard it said, "I know what I should be doing, and I want to do it, but I find I just can't." That's the story of my life, even as a child.

I knew the rules and wanted to keep them, but I just couldn't help myself. Then I tried to keep track of the rules I broke, because I was a legalistic little rule keeper. The older I got, the more rules there were. I either stressed myself out trying to keep them, or I failed and felt shame—over and over.

Have you ever gotten tired of the rules and wanted to do things your way? Frank Sinatra and many others proudly sang they did it their way. Regrets? They had a few, but so what? Well, plenty of times I tried doing things my way and have many regrets. I wonder how life could have been different had I stuck to the "good way" that I was taught as a child.

I grew up in church, learned Bible stories, believed in Jesus at an early age, and was baptized when I was sixteen years old. However, all the rules mandated by my church were hard to follow. Being holy or good had more to do with external things, like clothing or entertainment choices, rather than allowing God to change me from within.

No matter how hard I tried, I felt that God was disappointed in me and kept track of all my wrongdoings. I tried to keep track of them myself, but that was impossible. I loved Father God, but He seemed severe to me. Jesus wasn't proud of me either. For many years, I did my own thing by straying off the path of what was right. I experienced deep shame and regret because of my deeds and wasteful behavior.

When I turned eighteen, I decided to live on my own and make decisions based on my own rules. I did not make time for God or church. I married against my parents' wishes and thought I would live happily ever after. I wanted children, but that didn't happen. I was obsessed with trying to become pregnant. I bargained with God, wanting things *my way*. I would do this or that if He would just _____. Adoption seemed like the answer, and we spent a few years striving to make that happen. Eventually, two abused young sisters were placed in our home.

Adjusting to two new family members who had problems stemming from their backgrounds put an enormous strain on our marriage. Then my husband died suddenly. What a shock. Everything changed, and I was now alone. I couldn't keep the girls by myself, so I decided it would be best to place them in another home with both a mom and a dad.

I was truly alone. As I tried to find fulfillment, I drifted deeper into a pit, made bad decisions, and went through bad relationships. My mother was treated for leukemia, and my brother was diagnosed with a rare type of lymphoma.

The doctors determined that the best chance for my brother's survival was to have a bone marrow transplant. I was the perfect match to be his donor. God had prepared the way. My employer allowed me to take a leave of absence. I was single and had no responsibilities for others, and there was enough money to carry me through the months I'd be without paychecks.

We traveled to Seattle for the lengthy bone marrow transplant process. At that time, the surgery was extremely risky, and my brother's chances of recovery were not good. Through this experience, I was able to see God's hand at work. My brother's church family supported us with prayers and provided for our needs. It was a long ordeal, which was made more difficult by my mother's death, a devastating blow. However, on the day that my mother passed, my brother began his healing process. We saw his slow progress as a supernatural blessing from the Lord.

After meeting my future husband during these events, I returned home to marry and begin a life with him and his two children. I believed they were the answer to my needs, because I was so happy. I had what I thought I wanted. It was good, but my heart wasn't right. I longed for more for my husband and me.

One September morning in 1994, my life completely changed. As I listened to the radio and washed dishes, I heard the voices of little children singing about Jesus. I wondered, *What happened to me?* I was the little girl, then the teen, who loved Jesus, God's Son. Now I was the woman who was afraid to face

Him. I knew the only answer to my question was in God.

I stopped what I was doing, drove to the bookstore, and found a Bible study by Kay Arthur, *Lord, I Need Grace to Make It*. Immediately, I worked on the study and saw that grace didn't depend on trying to keep rules. The Bible made it clear that God loved me, and the only "work" I needed to do was simply believe what He said. I am saved by His grace—not by anything I do. My eyes were opened to realize I can never be separated from His love. I am forgiven.

In Colossians 2, I learned that He canceled the debt I owed, and there was peace between God and me. His Son, Jesus, paid for every bit of my debt on the cross. He forgave my sin, made me a new creature in Him, and gave me eternal life. No longer did I need to be afraid of death. The old me was buried with Him. After I gained a new understanding of these truths, I was re-baptized.

The day I discovered the Bible study, I attended church. That evening, the pastor extended an invitation to people who were struggling with addiction and had tried everything to quit but were unsuccessful. I went forward, believing this was my chance to do things God's way. The pastor asked me what I needed. I said, "To quit smoking." As he laid his hands on me to pray, I stopped him and said, "And I need joy and peace." That was it—a miracle. I was set free that day, and my heart was made right. The burden of guilt and shame lifted from me, and I have never had a desire for cigarettes since.

God changed me. As I studied His truth, I grew more confident in sharing my faith at work. I started a Bible study during lunch and had conversations with people who wanted to talk about God. Later, the attorney I worked with told me that what I shared with her had been a great positive influence.

God then gave me the opportunity for a new job at a Christian organization. I worked closely each day with a Bible teacher I had long admired. My work helped me grow in my walk. My compassion for others deepened, my ability to extend forgiveness increased, and I developed more patience and greater listening skills.

I am so thankful to God for opening my eyes to see His great love and faithfulness. In hindsight, I see the times when I made bad decisions and wrong turns, but the Lord worked those things for my good. My Father is so good and so faithful. What a great privilege to know He calls me His own. He's real and is here with me.

When you know Him, you know His voice. An example of this was the day my husband and I were on vacation, traveling from Georgia through the Smoky Mountains and on to Chicago. We were enjoying a wonderful fall trip and had just arrived in Gatlinburg, Tennessee. Who knew our visit to Tennessee would find us spending the next three days in the stroke unit at the University of Tennessee in Knoxville? I felt a check in my spirit that I should get upstairs to our hotel room. As I saw my husband's face and heard his voice change, I knew it was a stroke. I immediately called 9-1-1, and the paramedics helicoptered him to Knoxville.

I was left at the hotel with our luggage and thought, *Oh, God! I'm all alone again.* But no. I immediately heard the Holy Spirit reassure me, *You are not alone. I am with you.* God was in control of all the details. Everyone back home joined me and prayed for Jay. Everything turned out all right.

Over the years, I faced major difficulties with my husband's health, including stroke, heart attack, aneurism, and dementia. I faced cancer, as well as a very scary bout with a ruptured duodenal ulcer. We knew we were in God's hands, that He would take care of us and would see us through. I could not handle these things by myself, because all of them were out of my control.

Because God was in control, I was better able to handle crises. Seeing how miraculously He has worked in the past has given me confidence in Him for my future. Each time negative thoughts threaten me, telling me I may be alone again, I remember where I've been and the ways the Lord has gone before me and will always be with me. I know that all things work together for good as He works His plan.

My life changed for good the day I realized how great God's love is for me and that He created me to know Him. Just think. He wanted us to exist. That thrills me. The sins that separated me from Him were paid in full at the cross, and Jesus rising from the dead ensured my destination. Death won't be the end for me. I live for Him now and will live with Him one day in eternity. Until then, His Word and His Spirit are what cleanses and makes me holy—not following any manmade rules or traditions.

We must not wait to accept Jesus as Savior and Lord. The truth is, our lives can change in an instant. I know that from experience. I told my husband goodbye as he left for work one morning and received a call that afternoon to come to the hospital. I thought he had been in an accident. No. He had suffered a fatal heart attack.

We had no idea that morning what would happen later that day. The only goodbyes said were the usual "see you later." Everything came crashing down as I saw it all change and realized the brevity of our lives. The Bible says today is the day we must receive salvation for our sins and ensure our future forever. To refuse His call is to spend an eternity separated from God in darkness.

When I look back, I wonder, *Why did I fail so many times? How did I look away from what God had for me? How could I have been so blind?* I am encouraged by God's grace to share examples in the Bible of people who failed. We are dust, but in Christ we are strong when we fix our focus on Him and remember Who He is, what He has done, and what He has planned for us. Our failures will help us grow. His Word gives us hope.

Connie Steindorf left her home in Oklahoma to become a resident of Texas. Until December of 2019, when her husband, Jay, transitioned to Heaven, she enjoyed thirty-two years with him, their family, and grandchildren. Jay and Connie loved to snow and water ski and were blessed to visit Israel, Greece, Europe, Hawaii, Alaska, Canada, Mexico, and almost every state in the United States. Connie worked as a paralegal/legal assistant, as well as a research/administrative assistant to June Hunt at Hope for the Heart. She has been active in her church for thirty years and is a group leader for Bible Study Fellowship.

Thoughts to Ponder
from Breaking the Rules

1. When you stray, God wants you to come back to Him.

2. You are saved by His grace, not by anything you do.

3. Your life can change in an instant.

What rules have you broken?

For I do not do the good I want to do, but the evil I do not want to do—this I keep on doing. Thanks be to God, Who delivers me through Jesus Christ our Lord! — Romans 7:19, 25

Overcoming the Power of the Evil One

by Cathy Birungi

Sorcery. Betrayal. Demonic attacks. Snakes. Gangs. Coughing up blood. These are a part of my story. But thank God, these are not where it ends. My story is also one of miraculous redemption.

I was born in Uganda into a Muslim family. My father had six wives, and my mother was his first wife. She bore him four girls and one boy, of which I am the third oldest. My father was HIV positive and passed away when I was nine years old.

Life was a mess. We were denied our inheritance by other family members, and my mother didn't have a job to support us. This forced us all to work on other people's farms. Even though we had no inheritance, our family couldn't hinder us from attending cultural and Islamic ceremonies.

For a year, I stayed with my paternal great grandmother, who was a sorcerer. Being young, I didn't know that I was slated to become the next sorcerer in my generation. My great-granny, who was in her nineties, used her spiritual powers to treat people and earn a living. She was blind but had the spiritual ability to "see." She divined the exact number of clients who would come for treatment each day. Then she asked me to prepare the herbs and other necessities before their arrival.

Occasionally, I became sick. Rather than staying with my great-granny, I returned home to my mum. It was at that time I experienced demonic attacks. Also, strange snakes appeared in our home. Although the cause was unknown, our neighbors stopped socializing with us. My family elders believed that my late father and my younger twin brothers, who were dead, were visiting us as snakes, which appeared seasonally two months out of the year. Sometimes the snakes appeared when I was lying on the bed that I shared with my brother. When this happened, I was told to be calm. When the snakes appeared daily in a tie of three, we put the snakes to death. I realized later, after giving my life to Christ, that this was used by Him to help me conquer fear.

When I was sixteen, my uncle died. My family went to a distant area to bury him, and I was left at Granny's home to take care of my cousins. When it was time to go to sleep, I closed all the doors and windows. As soon as I reached my bed, with the door still closed, I heard footsteps. People opened the door to my room and sat on my bed. They stayed for a while, and when I turned to my other side, they left the room. I didn't sleep for the rest of the night.

Early the next morning, I felt the atmosphere of the attack, but I never told anyone about it for fear I would die. I called one of my cousins and told him I wasn't feeling well. I was so cold I went to the fireplace and tried in vain to get warm. Fortunately, my family arrived home. As I lost consciousness, I heard someone say, "You are going to fall into the fire." When I regained consciousness, they told me several demons spoke over me. Immediately, my family took me to the sorcerer in our village and sacrificed a hen's blood and herbs. I had no idea that they poured these into a cut in my flesh so they would seep into my blood. After that, I ceased eating meat, though presently I proudly and happily enjoy it.

When I turned seventeen, my mother could no longer afford the school fees for my siblings and me. Because my brother was a boy, she decided I should quit school instead of him. Because of the frequent demonic attacks, it was also difficult to continue my education. I became discouraged, joined a gang, went to night clubs, and developed bad habits. Nevertheless, being a Muslim girl, I still respected our norms and never drank alcohol or did drugs. People told me I wasn't the kind of person I was supposed to be. Many in my family hated me. I responded with arrogance and bitter speech, because I thought I had no other option. However, my mum never stopped giving me shelter or food.

I became like a mother to the other girls in my gang. I advised them not to drink too much, because they might be raped like other girls we knew. I also told them not to do drugs. I said, "Though we are firewood for Hell, we need life to live our life." As one amidst the flock, they took my word.

When I could see no future for me, I opted to get married

and quickly became pregnant. When I was two months along, I discovered that the man I married already had a wife and two children. I thought about this dilemma and considered an abortion. However, a friend of mine died while aborting, so I decided not to get an abortion.

I left my mum's home, because I didn't want her to realize I was pregnant. I got a job in town hawking drinking water from a retail shop. I rented a room and tried to hide my growing pregnancy. Six months later, I told my sister why I could no longer work. She took me back home, where I met my mum again. Though I expected a harsh welcome from my mother, her reaction was the opposite. She was happy to see me. In due time, I gave birth to a baby boy.

As my baby grew, I thought about how to earn a living. A friend who worked as a maid in Kampala said she could get me a job. I promised my son that he would never have to face the kind of life that I had. From then on, I quit thinking about myself and thought of my son.

I started working and met a Christian lady who became my good friend. She told me about Jesus the Son of God, took me to fellowship prayer meetings, and encouraged me to pray. I felt relieved by the atmosphere of the church. They praised God and sang worship songs. Through this, the burden that I had carried all my life was lifted. I regularly attended church with her, watched gospel programs on television, and listened to church services on the radio.

One time while watching a gospel program on television, the pastor asked those who wanted to give their lives to Jesus Christ to repeat the words that he said. I did what he asked and felt relief. When I told my friend, she was happy for me and told me I was now saved and was a born-again Christian. Even though she said this, I wondered, *What kind of God can forgive a person like me, who committed horrible sins?* When we went to church the next time, she told them I was a new convert. When one of the pastors prayed for me, I lost consciousness. Afterward, I was told that I fought them and that the spirits spoke through me saying I was the house of demons. The people prayed and freed me from the evil spirits. Since then, I have never had these attacks or lost consciousness.

I longed for God to forgive a person like me. Because I grew up in Islam, where good works such as praying five times a day, being welcoming and kind, and respecting Ramadan can save you, I believed I wasn't good enough to go to Heaven. This new message was so different from the one I learned when I was young. I was eager to read the Bible. Learning about Jesus and the miracles He performed brought me hope.

The preacher said those who believed in Christ and repented would go to Heaven, and those who didn't believe and repent would go to Hell. I didn't want my mother and siblings to go to Hell, so I tried to evangelize them. They told me to stop my nonsense, because I would cause more trouble when other family members heard of it. However, I never stopped praying that God would open their hearts to receive the gift of salvation.

I collected money and went with an evangelical team to my village, where we spent three days praying and preaching to my family and the community. We rejoiced when my mum received Jesus Christ as her personal God and Savior. Later, my siblings also joined us. Though this brought agony to my uncles and aunties, it never hindered my journey or stopped me from sharing Jesus. As bad as I previously was, I knew the transformative power of Jesus, and I was determined to be a good person and an overcoming Christian. This made my relatives upset, and they looked down on us even more.

Though I gave my life to Christ, I struggled for several years with unforgiveness toward my relatives for denying my mother a share of my late father's property. When my mum spoke up, one of my aunties bitterly slapped her in front of everyone. They forsook us and distributed the property among themselves and my father's other children.

The burden of unforgiveness became so great that it motivated me to work and earn money. I wanted to take revenge by suing them in court. I shared my plan with one of my pastors, but she said I had to forgive them and believe Christ for a new beginning. I didn't heed her advice, but I never stopped praying.

In my culture in Uganda, people went to church to spend the whole night in prayer. As I did this one night, I coughed, and blood spewed out of my mouth. Fortunately, some born-again

Christians who had come for their prayers immediately rushed me to a nearby clinic. Surprisingly, all the test results were negative, and the doctor assured us there was no immediate life-threatening problem that could cause severe bleeding. Because he thought I might have critical ulcers, he encouraged me to have an endoscopy.

While I was informing my boss about the issue, I coughed up blood again, even more severely than before. He was frightened and screamed for help. From there, I was rushed to the hospital for medical tests and treatment. Again the doctor found nothing wrong, and the endoscope test came back negative. My employer was so worried and fearful, he gave me a leave of absence and told me to go home and recover. Even though I had many tests, I knew that this was more than a physical disability. I stayed at my brother's house, and the attacks continued twice a day for seven days. My brother and I never stopped praying.

One night around midnight, I woke up and felt impressed to take Holy Communion. I read John 6:48–58, where Jesus says, "Whoever eats My flesh and drinks My blood remains in Me, and I in them." And, "The one who feeds on Me will live because of Me." As I took the bread, representing the body of Christ, and the juice, representing the blood of Christ, the Holy Spirit guided me to confess, *I eat of the bread from Heaven. I am not going to die.* I sensed the Holy Spirit saying, *Forgive. Forgive.* I felt bitter as I cried and confessed, *I forgive. I forgive my relatives and everyone who wronged me, and I forgive myself.* Then I fell asleep.

At sunrise the next day, my brother asked if I was well. I told him that I felt very weak. He said he was going to run a drip for me and went to his medical clinic to prepare. As soon as he left, I fell asleep. I had a vision in which I saw Jesus surrounded by a cloud of fire. He spoke commandingly to me. I saw a woman come out of my flesh, screaming as she flew away and then burst like sparks from a fire. Then I woke up. I happily called my brother and assured him I had been delivered. I told him about everything I saw. The blood flow stopped, and I was healed.

I thank God that my deliverance also caused my whole family to cease all kinds of evil practices. My auntie renounced my becoming the heir of sorcery. This was seconded by everyone in the family, and they destroyed all the sorcery materials my great-granny used, even though some of them are not yet believers. They called for reconciliation with the family, asked forgiveness from us, and willingly wanted to give us part of the share of our late father. Through the Holy Spirit's guidance, my brother and I did not accept and told them we did not need the land.

I continued to live with my brother. He had an idea about us starting an organization to save the lives of women who came to his clinic seeking an abortion. So we started a fellowship with the ladies and their children. We visited, encouraged, and strengthened them. The challenges we encountered earlier in our lives prepared us to answer the Lord's call by starting this ministry.

I now serve as a pastor in my brother's church, Passion Christian Assembly. I am also the Director of Latter Glory Outreach Foundation, which empowers women and young girls who are experiencing tragedy to receive a helping hand. This group teaches vocational skills like hairdressing, tailoring, and other courses. It pushes women to dream. My brother heads up Case Medical Centre.

I thank the Lord for the life that I now live. Christ is the reason that I can still breathe. He turned my shame into His glory. I am grateful for my mum and brother too, who never gave up on me. People say I am a good person, but it is only because of God's goodness that I have become who I am. He defeated the evil one and gave me life.

Cathy Birungi is a pastor in Kampala, Uganda. She was born into a Muslim family and came to Christ in 2005. As a single mother of one boy and caring for five other children, her passion is to reflect God's love in everything she does. With great joy, in October 2017, she opened Latter Glory Clinic. This clinic ministers to women who need maternity and medical care. Cathy can be contacted at **CathyBirungi02@gmail.com** *or* **www.LatterGloryClinic.org.**

Thoughts to Ponder

from Overcoming the Power of the Evil One

1. At the name of Jesus Christ,
    demons must flee.

2. God can rescue you from dire
    circumstances.

3. Forgiveness sets you free.

> **When have you overcome
> the power of the evil one?**

*You are strong, and the word of God lives in you,
and you have overcome the evil one. — 1 John 2:14*

Learning to Trust God
by Betty Willis

My story starts before I was born. My mama and daddy were
unequally yoked. Daddy was fun and charismatic, but not a
Christian. Mama thought she could change him. It was a source
of contention for their entire married life.

Mama was determined to raise her three children in church.
We walked every Sunday, because Daddy would not let us use
the pickup. My earliest memory is Daddy pulling us out of a
neighbor's car. The neighbor had stopped to offer us a ride.
Daddy said she could take us to church, but we had to walk.

Mama said marrying a non-Christian man was her biggest
mistake. There were problems from the beginning, but she was
against divorce because her parents had been divorced, and she
remembered the pain it caused her and her brothers and sisters.

In my opinion, all our lives would have been better if they
had divorced.

Mama took us to church every Sunday, against his wishes,
and we all became Christians and grew up to become active in
our churches.

Daddy owned a filling station/grocery store on a major
highway, which evolved into a wrecking yard/pawn shop. I was
pumping gas and selling peanut patties at a young age. We lived
in two rooms in the back of the store.

When I was in the second grade, I asked Daddy for a dollar
to buy a black patent leather purse with a shoulder strap. He
looked across the road and said, "You see those folks picking
cotton over there?"

"Yes, sir."

"You get yourself a cotton sack and pick enough cotton to
buy that purse."

I did and was extremely proud that I earned the money to
pay for the purse.

I started driving when I was ten years old. Daddy always had
old wrecked cars that he allowed me to drive to school. On the
way, I picked up my friends. Having a car made me popular
with the other kids.

When I turned sixteen, I got my driver's license so I could legally drive on the main roads. This also enabled me to get a job at a church camp twenty miles away. I went on Tuesday nights, stayed in a cabin on the grounds, worked the rest of the week until Sunday afternoon, and then drove home.

My first chore was at five in the morning when I broke about 300 eggs to be scrambled. Then I did whatever the older ladies told me to do. I served the teenagers and cleaned up the kitchen. At ten in the morning, two in the afternoon, and nine o'clock at night, I opened the canteen and sold cold drinks and candy to the teenage campers. I also helped with lunch and supper.

Working while kids my age were playing was embarrassing.

One late Sunday afternoon, I was driving my old wrecked car home from camp when the radiator started smoking and two tires blew out. I walked to a nearby house to use their phone to ask Daddy to come to get me.

He said, "Is the car still running?"

With tears rolling down my cheeks, I said, "Yes, but two of the tires are flat, and it's smoking like crazy."

"Does it still have wheels?"

"Yes."

"Then come on home." He did not want to come and get me.

When I graduated from high school, everybody talked about where they were going to college. My English teacher said I had writing talent and encouraged me to go to Texas Christian University in Fort Worth. I went home and told Mama and Daddy.

Daddy said, "Who's going to pay for it?"

I said, "Well, I thought you would."

"I'm not paying for it."

"If you sign these papers, I can get a loan to go to college."

"I'm not signing any papers."

"What am I supposed to do?"

He said, "You go up to that department store and get a job selling shoes or something, and pretty soon you'll be the manager. You don't need to go to college."

Mama was sitting quietly in the corner. "What about that nice Willis boy who keeps hanging around here? Why don't you

212

marry him? He comes from a good Christian family."

I wasn't desperately in love with Jack Willis, but I married him that summer. About five years later, I realized I loved him. Mama was right! We had three children, a girl and two boys. Our marriage has been good, and by the grace of God, we will soon be married sixty-two years.

Daddy died young, due to smoking two packs of cigarettes a day from the time he was thirteen. His death was horrible because of emphysema. He drowned because of fluid in his lungs. His last words were, "I'd give anything for another cigarette."

About five years before his death, Daddy made a profession of faith and accepted Jesus as his Savior.

When we went through his billfold, we found a letter I had written to him about ten years before. It said I wanted to thank him for teaching me to be independent and strong. I also told him I liked double-mint gum and licorice because of him. I couldn't believe he had carried that letter around for so long.

Mama said her life began the day he died.

One stormy afternoon, my brother and Mama were sitting in the living room. My brother said, "Mama, didn't Pop say he was going to hide some money around here somewhere?"

She said, "Oh, he used to kid around that he was going to hide some behind that door facing over there."

Daddy didn't trust banks, because he was raised during the depression. My brother pulled the facing off and behind it was ten thousand dollars neatly folded.

Mama clapped her hands. "Hot dog, we're going to the Holy Land." And we did!

Mama had always dreamed of seeing places mentioned in the Bible and walking where Jesus walked. Daddy told her that was silly and never allowed her to go. I figured Daddy was rolling in his grave, but we had a ball!

In summary, the nutshell version of my early life is that Daddy taught me independence and a good work ethic. Mama taught me about Jesus and helped me begin my journey of learning to trust God.

In the 1960s, money was tight for my husband and me. He worked hard but made just enough to pay rent, utilities, and food. I took care of the three kids and tried to make do. Ten dollars a week was all we could afford for groceries. There was no extra money.

When my youngest was ten, I decided I needed to find a job. First, I worked part-time at our church as a secretary. The kids walked over to the church when they got home from school, and I walked home with them. Because I wasn't earning much, I prayed for a better-paying job. I confided in a church member friend that I was looking for work that paid more. He said I needed to talk to his best friend, who was a real estate broker.

I got my license and loved real estate. I was the top producer for over twenty-five years, and my loyal clients still call me today. Most of my clients were from our church and the local college.

These experiences helped me inch forward on my journey of learning to trust God.

However, it wasn't until about thirty years ago that I learned how to effectively communicate with God. This was when my faith-walk rapidly accelerated.

I learned that once I accepted Jesus as my Savior, I had instant access to more than eight thousand promises, but I had to claim them. Promises such as:

- He will be with me in all situations.
- I don't have to be anxious.
- I can trust in Him, and He will direct my ways.
- He wants me to know His will for my life more than I want to know it.

Jesus said you have not because you ask not. Also, ask and it will be given to you. Seek and you will find. Knock and it will be opened unto you.

We need to walk in His ways and spend time with Him daily by praying and reading the Bible. For me, the best time to commune with God is early in the morning. When I wake up to go to the bathroom around five o'clock, I stay up. You might say my bladder is God's alarm clock. I flip on the coffee pot, then go straight to my "prayer chair," an old overstuffed reupholstered chair. Kneeling, I put my elbows and head in the chair and talk to God. I use the following format for prayer:

I praise Him and thank Him for dying on the cross for my sins. I thank Him for my health and pray for my family and friends by name.

I confess my known sins to Him and ask for forgiveness. For me, this always includes my lack of patience, forgiving others, taming my tongue, and not trusting Him more.

I lay out my petitions to Him. Specific needs for myself and others, and I pray for our government.

I thank Him in advance for His answers and ask that the answers will be according to His will.

I ask Him to nudge me if I am to act.

Then I get a cup of coffee, sit in my recliner, and spend about thirty minutes reading the Bible. I use a day-by-day guide that takes me through the Bible in a year.

Learning to better communicate and trust God has prepared me for difficult seasons in my life.

One June, I was driving down a major city street and glanced at a billboard about mammograms. I had a strong impression that I needed to get a mammogram. I had not been to a doctor in almost two years.

Immediately, I drove to the medical building and told the receptionist I needed a mammogram. She knew me and said, "Well, Mrs. Willis, we are scheduling two months out, but I will be happy to set you an appointment." While she was leafing through her appointment book, the phone rang. The call was from someone who could not keep her appointment, because of a personal emergency. The receptionist hung up the phone and said, "We can take you right now. We just had a cancellation."

Ladies, you know how fun mammograms are. You feel like you are being squished between two bricks. After the procedure, the nurse inspected the x-rays and then called for a second opinion. They both agreed I needed a sonogram.

They slathered me with sticky goo, then performed the sonogram. The doctor came in, reviewed the x-rays and sonogram, and said, "Betty, you have a tiny suspicious lump. We need to send you to the surgeon to get a biopsy."

Three days after the biopsy, a nurse called. The tissue was malignant, and I was going to need a lumpectomy. I agreed. The resulting lumpectomy report said the margins weren't clear, so they did another lumpectomy. The margins were still not clear. My breast was beginning to look a little lop-sided. The doctor said I had "options." What a word! He meant I could have thirty-three zaps of radiation and chemotherapy or I could have a mastectomy.

I told him I would pray about it and let him know. I shared the information with my husband and daughter. However, I needed my mama, who was then ninety-five years old.

Mama and I had a close relationship. In the previous five years, we became even closer as I visited often, and she shared stories of her childhood. We had a good time documenting the stories and I compiled a book called *Ruby Remembers*. Initially, I printed 500 copies, mainly for the family, but we sold them quickly. Mama loved the book and was extremely proud to be "Pioneer Woman of Hill County."

She was a committed Christian and sharp as a tack. Everyone in the family went to her for prayer and advice on important matters. After she heard about my situation, she prayed with me and asked if I had been saying my Bible verses about not worrying and knowing God cares for me. When I cried, she said, "We have to sing." So we sang "Standing on the Promises," "Count your Blessings," and other songs from our old green hymnal about trusting God. Every night at nine o'clock, I called her. We prayed, said our affirming verses, and sang.

I was still working, and it was 100 degrees most days that summer. The doctors took me off hormones as soon as they suspected cancer, so I was having one hot flash after another. My body wanted its estrogen. I was still trying to decide what to do.

I talked to lots of women who had been diagnosed with breast cancer. Some had radiation and chemotherapy. Others had mastectomies. Everybody had an opinion, but I didn't feel peace with any of them. By this time, I shared the news about my breast cancer diagnosis with my Christian friends. A lot of people were praying for me.

On August 13, Mama turned ninety-six.

On September 1, Mama had a lung embolism. A blood clot went to her lung. In the hospital, she had severe shortness of breath, so they put an oxygen mask on her. Her skin appeared gray.

Someone from our family, including my brother, sister, nine grandchildren, and me, stayed with her every minute she was in the hospital. We sang and read scriptures and rubbed her arms and legs with lotion.

One morning, I was sitting with Mama when the doctor came in and said, "Mrs. Schulz, do you know who I am?"

She said, "Sure, you're Doctor Earhart."

"I have some hard questions to ask you. If you can't eat, do you want us to feed you through a tube in your stomach?"

"No."

He said, "If your heart stops, do you want us to start it again?"

"No. I am old enough to die."

He looked at me.

I nodded slightly and shrugged. She had made her decision.

When he left, I lay beside her with my arm over her and whispered in her ear. "Mama, you are so brave. Please don't leave me. We all depend on you to pray for us and guide us."

She said, "I think it's your turn."

She didn't talk much after that. She became weaker, kept her eyes closed, and refused to eat. We swabbed her mouth and tried to get her to eat soup or drink juice or water, but she refused. Her skin became increasingly gray. My sister says that when older people decide to die, they starve themselves. I think that might be true.

Most of the time, I stayed at night and lay in bed with her. One night she asked what I was doing about my cancer. I said, "Nothing, I am still praying about it."

By the middle of October, the doctors convinced me to make an appointment to start radiation treatments.

One morning, I was sitting with Mama. It was around noon. I was reading with my back to the windows, basking in the warm sunshine. Suddenly, I didn't hear Mama gasping. I looked up to see she had taken the oxygen mask off and was smiling at me. The sun was on her face and her clear blue eyes were bright. I could not see a wrinkle.

I said, "Well, hello there."

She kept smiling and said clearly, "You are going to be all right. Just trust in the Lord, and He will lead you."

I jumped up to hug her, but by the time I got there, she was gray and gasping again.

That afternoon, someone came to stay with Mama while my daughter and I went to a little dress shop near the hospital. My daughter was looking for a special banquet dress, and my job was to approve or disapprove as she modeled her selections.

A young woman came and sat down beside me, and we chit-chatted.

She said, "I am a widow."

I said, "Honey, you sure are young to be a widow."

"I know. My husband had breast cancer right here, and the radiologist cooked his heart." The place she pointed to was exactly where my cancer was.

I rushed to the dressing room and asked my daughter to come out and meet her. She and I went back to the place where the woman and I were sitting, but there was no one there! I searched the shop and asked the girls at the checkout counter if they had seen her. They said no, they hadn't seen a woman like that. I was a little freaked by the experience, but I decided to keep my radiation appointment the next morning.

I didn't sleep much that night and prayed that God would be with me. The next morning my husband went with me to the cancer center.

The nurse put me in a hospital gown, had me lie down in a tray, and put a permanent dot tattoo on my stomach. She could have at least made it a butterfly. She explained that the dot was for a reference point for each of the thirty-three radiation zaps.

The radiologist came in, asked me to put my right arm over my head, and pulled the gown down to expose my breast. As he started lining up the light over my head, the door burst open and a local community college teacher came in, along with two students, a boy and a girl. She laughed and said, "You don't mind if we observe, do you?"

Well, I did mind, but I didn't say anything. She didn't give me a chance to answer anyway. I listened to her talk to the students, and she said, "Now when he flips that switch over there, that's when the radiation is working, and we'll want to get behind this lead screen, because we don't want any of that to get on us."

That is when God showed up. I was impressed that I should not proceed with the radiation treatments. I said to the radiologist, "Don't touch that switch, I'm getting up."

The instructor looked at her students and said, "This usually doesn't happen."

I quickly dressed and left. When I entered the waiting room, my husband said, "That didn't take long."

I said, "God told me not to have it done. Let's go home."

Although I realize radiation is an effective and appropriate treatment for many cancer patients, I believe, without a doubt, that God was telling me to make another choice.

On October 30, Mama died.

The day after Mama's funeral, I had a double mastectomy. I came to the clear conclusion that I could never trust my breast tissue again. For me, a double mastectomy with reconstruction was the way to go.

That has been fourteen years ago, and I am satisfied with my decision. I am alive, and I can wear bathing suits and low-cut blouses, with cleavage. Even better, I never have to have another mammogram.

Mama was right. I trusted in the Lord, and He led me.

Betty Willis is a Christian realtor and historical fiction author from Waco, Texas. She is employed by Coldwell Banker Apex. Betty documented her mother's life in the book, Ruby Remembers. *Her second award-winning novel,* Mattie, *is based on the life of her dyslexic grandmother. Betty is just finishing a novel called,* Texas Quest, *about German immigrants who came to Texas in 1870. She is active in the Waco community, a prison volunteer, and attends First Baptist Woodway. Betty and her husband, Jack, enjoy traveling and Baylor sports. Email Betty at* **BettyWillis@hot.rr.com.**

Thoughts to Ponder

from Learning to Trust God

1. Daily prayer and Bible reading build trust in God.

2. God can communicate with you in many ways.

3. The Bible has thousands of promises available to believers.

What experiences have helped you trust God more fully?

Trust in the Lord with all your heart and lean not on your own understanding; in all your ways submit to Him, and He will make your paths straight. — Proverbs 3:5–6

Anti-Virus Protection

by Juanita Williams

What does a computer do to reach the Internet? It gets connected. For a connection to be established, a modem and a network information card are necessary. Users can cause their computer to become infected by a malware virus if they are tricked into clicking and/or installing a program they should not. Users might not know right away that their operating system is affected until it starts showing signs (e.g. slowing down, popping up ads, etc.). This malicious code executes actions that the user doesn't anticipate or intend. It can also prevent connection to the Internet, sometimes forcing the user to make a payment to regain access. It is designed to reproduce itself and spread from one file or program to another.

Similar to how a computer virus spreads, once it has access to a vulnerable operating system, the virus of sin was spread to all humanity by the serpent. He tricked the first human parents into thinking that if they disobeyed God, their operating system would function better, and they would have full control over how it functions. However, Adam and Eve did not realize that their decision to receive the lie broke their perfect connection with God. The main goal of the sin virus was to control and prevent us from realizing that we live disconnected from the One Who created us with His purpose in mind. Let me share how this virus operated in my life to accomplish its goal.

Growing up, I was not connected to my parents. My mom left when I was five. I remember seeing her three times after she left my father: when she kidnapped us from our aunt's house, when we saw her briefly downtown with my dad and his girlfriend, and when she visited us at our home to tell us that she loved us. My brothers and I were raised by our father. Our home was tumultuous, because my father was an alcoholic and had mental health problems. Although I was angry with my father, I still attempted to please him by getting good grades, doing the right things, and being responsible.

The connection that I had with my best friend, Cheryl Nelson, was broken right before my thirteenth birthday. She was moving away, because her father was killed that morning. I was shocked, saddened, and lost as I went through my school day. When I came home from school, my world was rocked even further. I was told that my mom had been killed by a drunk driver—one of my dad's good friends.

I still remember the headlines in our local paper. Once the shock wore off, rage and guilt consumed me. I was enraged by the man who killed my mom. I was also riddled with guilt, because she had come to our home late the night before and told me she loved me. I said, "Yeah, okay, I love you too. Now let me get some sleep." I cannot rewind the clock to that moment. I wondered if I had awakened enough to have a conversation with her, would she have died that night? I had so many questions that she wouldn't be able to answer.

Over the years, I realized how much I lost. She did not see me as a woman looking just like her. She missed my wedding and meeting her grandchildren. The drunk driver robbed me of an opportunity to have a relationship with my mother. I thought, *Why is he still alive?* I wanted him dead rather than my mom. Seeing him again after his short time in prison was too much. Unforgiveness, abandonment, confusion, and hopelessness infected my operating system.

About six months after my mother's death, my hero aunt became extremely ill. She had been there for my two brothers and me when my father was at work or unable to care for us. I loved going to her house and having sweet and creamy coffee after school. I enjoyed it when she went to the drive-in movies with us. However, my father paid the kid's price for her, because she looked so young. She was one of the strongest women I knew.

When I was fifteen, she died. Another loss. I had mixed emotions of dread, hopelessness, and relief, because she suffered greatly as cancer took over her body. I recall my last visit to her hospital room. She was in a coma, and her mouth was open. I still remember the awful smell and how this disease had its way in her. When she succumbed to cancer, my father went into a deeper pit of instability. This was a breaking point for our family. *Who would have my back? Who would be there for my dad and my brothers?* This loss was more than we could bear. We

222

did not know how to fix this hurt and pain.

These losses were downloaded into my processing system and caused me to look for fixes to operate properly. These attempts kept me trapped in various addictions as I navigated through the turbulent waters of circumstances that I did not understand. I was angry and blamed God, Whom I did not know, for allowing this pain and confusion in my life. Why would He allow me to experience all this pain? Have you at some point in your life asked the same question? I couldn't receive His love or respond to others who desired to love me.

Another headline in a newspaper about my cousin's best friend, Freddie Nixon, helped me move closer to discovering how this virus affected my life. He was popular in his hometown and came to stay with us for a brief period after he was diagnosed with leukemia. A reporter asked if he had a fear of dying. He said he was not afraid to die, because he knew where he was going. He died shortly after the article was written, and there was a home-going service for him. That service was a celebration of his life, not a sad occasion like other funerals I had attended.

His death caused me great distress. Because we were in our twenties, I felt like it was too young to die from a disease. The peace that he had about leaving this world challenged and intrigued me, and I wanted to know what his secret was. This set off a lot of questions in my mind, because dying was one of my fears. I wanted to have the security he seemed to have about dying. My frustrations mounted professionally and relationally during this time, and it drove me to search for a fix for the things wrong within me.

While on this search, my resident manager asked if I wanted joy. She shared with me that true joy can only be found in Jesus Christ. All I had to do was trust what she was sharing with me about God. Adam and Eve, the first human parents, allowed the virus of sin to infect their operating system. Their attempts to fix it was to run, cover themselves up, and hide from God. Their relationship was negatively affected, and their hiding from God implies that they did not view God or each other in the same way as before. God came looking for them, but they did not move toward Him. When I attempted to cover my shame and guilt, God asked me the same question He asked Adam and Eve. "Where are you?" The covering I attempted did not bring the healing that I needed to be rightly connected to God or others.

Adam and Eve also did not take responsibility for allowing the virus into their system. They played the blame game. Eve's fix was to blame the serpent. Adam's fix was to blame God for the woman that He gave him, who caused him to eat from the forbidden tree. I too, like Adam, was infected with the sin virus and blamed God for not stopping all the challenging experiences that occurred in my life.

God allowed His Son Jesus to take the penalty for our sins by dying, although He was sinless. He loves us that much. Just as He originally intended, He endured shame and suffered for each one of us so we could be connected to Him. I admitted that I had a sin problem and asked Christ into my heart. At that moment, the virus was removed, and I received my new operating system. It allowed me to process the new information that I had been lost but now was found.

With the virus removed and believing that my fix was found in God, I received the best antivirus protection program in the person of the Holy Spirit. He continually roots out new virus attempts, detects, and warns me of what should be done. I now have the power to respond to infections that earlier kept me disconnected from God and others.

He has protected me against any virus that attempts to corrupt my operating system. This fix has allowed me to see that my system was infected with anger, unforgiveness, hopelessness, fear, frustration, guilt, shame, and condemnation, and kept me searching for security, stability, and safety. Jesus showed me that I can trust Him with my insecurities and that He has designed me to connect and stay connected to Him. Jesus did not leave me in a lost state, but came to me and received me.

Being connected to Jesus allowed me to recognize several things. First, there was purpose in my pain. Jesus desired that I love Him more than I desired to have what I perceived to be the perfect family. His provision and planning brought me to where I am. I no longer believed the lie that God was not good because of the pain I endured. Have I grieved what I lost?

Absolutely! However, I realize that Jesus Christ came to Earth and identified with my hurt and pain. There was purpose in His pain as He came to Earth and endured a humiliating and horrific death to destroy the virus of evil.

Second, Jesus demonstrated to me His forgiveness toward me, which helped me recognize that I needed to take responsibility for my actions and ask others to forgive me. It also allowed me to extend forgiveness to the man who killed my mom. It took me years to release the bitterness I held in my heart toward him for taking my mom away.

A co-worker's son killed two people while drunk, and I had the opportunity to witness the torment he was living in. He lived in his own hell. He shared with me that he did not remember the details of that night, nor could he sleep peacefully. Even after being released from jail, his life was on a downward trajectory. It was then I realized that the man that killed my mom was probably tormented as well.

I found that to be true when my father called to tell me that that the drunk driver, who killed my mom, came by the house and told my father how he wanted to kill himself. As I listened, I said, "Dad, I'm so sorry that he wants to kill himself. Please tell him that I forgive him." I allowed him to write to me. Within a year, he was found dead in a park. My father believes he succeeded in killing himself. Have you or do you feel like I did, blaming God for your pain? Have you believed the lie that God will not forgive you? Are you having a hard time forgiving yourself?

Third, I cannot live my life disconnected from Jesus. The Lord sweetly ministered to me regarding my fear of dying like my mom and grandmom, who both died before they were forty years old. He gave me the verse, "I will not die but live, and will proclaim what the Lord has done" (Psalm 118:17). I am now fifty years old. He kept this promise to me. I have been able to declare His works with my children and others that He has put in my path. Had I not gone through life-altering challenges, I would not have recognized my need for Him.

The threats against my operating system do not stop. I am so glad to know that the Holy Spirit performs a scan so I can understand how I respond to circumstances that affect me. God wanted to reestablish His connection with me. He wants to connect with you too—just ask.

Juanita Williams is Cofounder of FourThirTeen Youth Ministry. She utilizes her passion by advocating, inspiring, educating, empowering, and mentoring adolescent girls. She shepherds women and children through her leadership at church, school, and community. Juanita enjoys time with family, friends, exercising, reading, and writing. She is a counseling student at Dallas Theological Seminary and expects to graduate in December 2020. Juanita and her husband, Charles, have been married 22 years. They are marriage mentors through their local church and are the proud parents of four children: Chaz, Naomi, Nathaniel, and Cymone. In her spare time, Juanita blogs at **https://PerspectivesOnMyPilgrimage.wordpress.com**. *Her email address is* **JuanitaWilliamsLVD@gmail.com.**

Thoughts to Ponder
from Anti-Virus Protection

1. Sin disconnects you from God.

2. Attempting to hide from God will not eliminate your feelings of guilt and shame.

3. True joy only comes from Jesus.

What pain do you need to give to Jesus?

The wages of sin is death, but the gift of God is eternal life in Christ Jesus our Lord. — Romans 6:23

Beliefs from God's Word

We believe . . . the Bible is the verbally inspired Word of God and without mistakes as originally written. It is the complete revelation of His will for salvation and the only unfailing rule of faith and practice for the Christian life.

We believe . . . in one God, Creator of all things, eternally existing in three persons: Father, Son, and Holy Spirit, and that these three are co-eternal and of equal dignity and power.

We believe . . . in the deity of Jesus Christ, His miraculous conception by the Holy Spirit, His virgin birth, His sinless life; His substitutionary death on a cross, His bodily resurrection, His ascension to the right hand of the Father, and His personal, imminent return.

We believe . . . that man was created by and for God. By man's disobeying God, every person incurred spiritual death, which is separation from God and physical death. All people are sinners by nature and practice.

We believe . . . the Lord Jesus Christ died for our sins, and all who believe in Him are declared righteous because of His sacrificial death and are, therefore, in right relationship with God.

We believe . . . in the present ministry of the Holy Spirit indwelling all believers and thus enabling and empowering the life and ministry of the believer.

We believe . . . in the bodily resurrection of everyone who has lived, the everlasting blessedness of those in right relationship with God, and the everlasting punishment of those who have rejected God's forgiveness in His Son.

God's Good News for You

Now that you have read these stories of great faith, you may want to know how you can have this same kind of faith. We have Good News for you.

He loves you!

For God so loved the world that He gave His one and only Son, that whoever believes in Him shall not perish but have eternal life. — John 3:16

He wants to meet your need.

Your iniquities have separated you from your God; your sins have hidden His face from you, so that He will not hear. — Isaiah 59:2

God made Him Hho had no sin to be sin for us, so that in Him we might become the righteousness of God. — 2 Corinthians 5:21

He offers you a free gift!

The wages of sin is death, but the gift of God is eternal life in Christ Jesus our Lord. — Romans 6:23

How to receive this gift:

If you declare with your mouth, "Jesus is Lord," and believe in your heart that God raised Him from the dead, you will be saved. — Romans 10:9

Jesus, I recognize I have sinned and need You. I believe You are the Son of God, that You died on the cross for my sin, rose from the dead and now sit at the right hand of God. I trust You alone and choose to follow You. Thank You for forgiving me of my sin and giving me eternal life. In Jesus' name, amen.

If you have chosen to receive God's gift or would like more information, please contact us at **info@RoaringLambs.org**. We would love to hear from you!

Share with Us

Roaring Lambs is working on the next volume of *Stories of Roaring Faith*. These stories are designed to lead a non-believer to faith in Jesus Christ, as well as encourage followers of Jesus. We would love to receive your testimony.

The guidelines for submission include:

- A typed and double-spaced story with approximately 3,000 words.
- An 80-100-word bio with contact information that you want published.
- A signed Release Form, which is found at ***RoaringLambs.org/Share-Your-Story***.
- A title, three lessons learned, key scripture, and one question for readers to contemplate.
- Submitting everything to ***Info@RoaringLambs.org***.

Also, you may be invited as a guest to our radio show, *A Time to Dream*, which features life-changing testimonies.

Let God use your story by writing, sending, and sharing what He has done for you.

Support Us

Roaring Lambs Ministries is a 501(c)(3), which exists on tax-deductible donations. We welcome any gifts to sustain our ministry in equipping believers to better communicate their faith. Donate online at ***RoaringLambs.org/Donate*** or mail checks to:

Roaring Lambs
17110 Dallas Pkwy Ste 260
Dallas, TX 75248

There are other ways to give to Roaring Lambs: gifts of stock, real estate, or planned gifts by will or trust. Roaring Lambs can help you by working with your attorney or accountant.

Give, and it will be given to you. A good measure, pressed down, shaken together and running over, will be poured into your lap. For with the measure you use, it will be measured to you. — *Luke 6:38*

Acknowledgments

My sincere thanks are extended to Frank Ball for his gracious help turning this manuscript into a book. You are a kind, generous, God-loving man, and much appreciated by this ministry.

To Dan Thompson, our graphic designer from T-Bone Designs. Many thanks for all your work with Roaring Lambs, to give us such a great look. You are talented and have established our visual image. Thanks especially for a great cover for this book.

Thank you, Sherry Ryan, for your work editing the testimonies. I know you were blessed by reading them, but we are blessed by all your spelling, punctuation, grammar corrections, and understanding of how to create an effective testimony story.

To my partner in ministry, Belinda McBride, without you, this book would have never been completed. Thank you for your endless hours of reading and re-reading the stories. Thank you for your attention to the small details. Thank you for your heart for this project and all the things we do at Roaring Lambs. You are a gift from God to this ministry.

Thank you, again, to all who contributed their testimonies. This book is not about you but all about the great and awesome God we serve.

About the Editors

Donna Skell

With a heart for God, people, and business, Donna stays active in the Christian community. She has been involved with this ministry since its inception and came on staff in 2008. Donna oversees all Roaring Lambs events and Bible studies. She co-hosts an international radio show called *A Time to Dream*, airing four times a week on three platforms. The program features powerful faith stories. By collecting these amazing stories, Roaring Lambs has now produced five volumes of *Stories of Roaring Faith*. She especially enjoys speaking to ladies' groups, churches, and retreats. Her rich Jewish heritage and her study of God's Word enhance her insight into the issues involved in Christian faith and living. In addition to her work with Roaring Lambs, Donna serves on the Christian Women in Media Advisory Committee, and the Collin County Christian Prayer Breakfast Committee. **DSkell@RoaringLambs.org**

Belinda McBride

Answering God's call at age nine to become a "missionary," Belinda's mission was to reach others with the Good News of Jesus Christ. Today her passion is to equip believers to effectively live life with hope, purpose, and strength. She does this as a pastor's wife, administrator, Bible study teacher, speaker, and writer.

Belinda has served in many churches and ministries, including Hope for the Heart, Marketplace Chaplains, and Roaring Lambs. Belinda's great joy is her husband, four daughters, sixteen grandchildren, and one great-granddaughter. She currently resides in Carrollton, Texas, and is Director of Operations with Roaring Lambs. Contact her at **BMcBride@RoaringLambs.org.**

Dr. Sherry Ryan

Dr. Ryan is a retired Associate Professor of Information Technology and Decision Sciences at the University of North Texas. She received her Ph.D. in Information Systems from the University of Texas at Arlington and an MBA from the University of Southern California. Prior to earning her doctorate, she worked for IBM, teaching courses and speaking at national conferences.

She has published numerous academic journal articles, conference proceedings, and is currently working on a book. Sherry has two children, one granddaughter, and one grandson. She manages the Roaring Lambs website, is passionate about missions, and is on the Board of Directors for "His Appointed Time Ministries."

Ministry@RoaringLambs.org

Frank Ball

For ten years, Frank Ball directed North Texas Christian Writers to help members improve their writing and storytelling skills. In 2011, he founded Story Help Groups and joined the Roaring Writers ministry seven years later to encourage and equip all Christians to tell their life-changing stories.

He has taught at writer's conferences and churches across the U.S. and Canada. Besides writing his own books, he does ghostwriting, copy editing, and graphic design to help others publish high-quality books.

As Pastor of Biblical Research and Writing for three years, he wrote sermons, teaching materials, and hundreds of devotions. He coaches writers, writes blogs, and is a panelist on The Writer's View. His first book, *Eyewitness: The Life of Christ Told in One Story*, is a compilation of biblical information on the life of Christ in a chronological story that reads like a novel. His website is **FrankBall.org**.

FBall@RoaringLambs.org

Made in the USA
Columbia, SC
29 October 2020